C000232715

RUSSIA'S
CIVIL WAR

RUSSIA'S
CIVIL WAR

Geoffrey Swain

TEMPUS

First published 2000

PUBLISHED IN THE UNITED KINGDOM BY:

Tempus Publishing Ltd
The Mill, Brimscombe Port
Stroud, Gloucestershire GL5 2QG

PUBLISHED IN THE UNITED STATES OF AMERICA BY:

Tempus Publishing Inc.
2 Cumberland Street
Charleston, SC 29401
(Tel: 1-888-313-2665)

Tempus books are available in France, Germany and Belgium
from the following addresses:

Tempus Publishing Group	Tempus Publishing Group	Tempus Publishing Group
21 Avenue de la République	Gustav-Adolf-Straße 3	Place de L'Alma 4/5
37300 Joué-lès-Tours	99084 Erfurt	1200 Brussels
FRANCE	GERMANY	BELGIUM

© Geoffrey Swain, 2000

The right of Geoffrey Swain to be identified as the Author
of this work has been asserted by him in accordance with the
Copyrights, Designs and Patents Act 1988.

All rights reserved. No part of this book may be reprinted or reproduced or utilised in
any form or by any electronic, mechanical or other means, now known or hereafter
invented, including photocopying and recording, or in any information storage or
retrieval system, without the permission in writing from the Publishers.

British Library Cataloguing in Publication Data.
A catalogue record for this book is available from the British Library.

ISBN 0 7524 1790 8

Typesetting and origination by Tempus Publishing.
PRINTED AND BOUND IN GREAT BRITAIN.

To the memory of Roger Pethybridge,
a good scholar and a good friend

Contents

List of illustrations

Reproduced by permission of:

* ⋆   Latvian War Museum, Riga
* ⋆⋆ Private collection of Valdis Berzins
* †   Private collection of Beryl Williams

Colour plates

Glossary

All sides in Russia's civil war tried to establish representative assemblies to which they were responsible in some way. These are most logically catalogued by year:

1917

As a counterweight to the soviets, which only represented the working population, it was agreed in August to summon the **Moscow State Conference**, which would allow representatives from all social classes of Russia to express their views; it was preceded by the **Meeting of Civic Figures**, an assembly of the old elites, and followed in September by the **Democratic Conference** which, like the soviets, only represented the working classes. The **Preparliament** was summoned in October, as a temporary body giving representation to all classes. In November elections were finally held to the **Constituent Assembly**, Russia's first democratic parliament.

1918

The Bolshevik dispersal of the Constituent Assembly prompted their SR opponents to call their first anti-Bolshevik administration the Committee of the Constituent Assembly, or **Komuch**. After talks brokered by the Allies and the moderate Union for the Regeneration of Russia, representatives of Komuch and the rival anti-Bolshevik administrations of the Urals and Siberia met, at the **Chelyabinsk State Conference** and the **Ufa State Conference**, to form the **Directory**, the anti-Bolshevik administration the Allies were prepared to recognize. Admiral Kolchak staged his coup against the Directory on 18 November. The coup was prompted by the Directory's success in challenging the powers of the **Administrative Council**, the secretive committee through which reactionaries in the Siberian Government had sought to prevent both the Constituent Assembly and the **Siberian Regional Assembly**, which post-dated it, exercising any democratic control over the anti-Bolshevik movement.

1919

Admiral Kolchak established a **State Economic Conference** as a consultative body from which to draw the views of financiers and industrialists; his opponents in Siberia campaigned to establish a **Land Assembly** as a democratic alternative, and formed the **Political Centre** to coordinate their struggle. General Denikin called his advisory assembly the **Special Council**; some of his opponents established the Committee for the Liberation of the Black Sea Coast, **KOCh**, as a representative assembly for those trying to depose him.

A Note on the SRs

The Party of Socialist Revolutionaries, or **SRs**, believed in the socialist instincts of the Russian peasantry and wanted to turn Russia into a democratic federation. The party split in October 1917 over whether to continue to support a coalition government with the liberals or whether to help establish a soviet government, a coalition of the socialist parties (Bolsheviks, Mensheviks and SRs) represented in the soviets. The **Left SRs** supported the Bolsheviks until the Treaty of Brest Litovsk was signed with Germany. When, by summer 1918, the Bolsheviks had established their one-party dictatorship, the differences between the Left SRs and other SRs narrowed; those SRs who still favoured cooperation with the liberals formed the **Union for the Regeneration of Russia**. The **Narod Group** of SRs, established in 1919, favoured cooperation with the Bolsheviks in the struggle against Admiral Kolchak and General Denikin. In 1919 the majority of SRs in Ukraine adopted the name **Borotbists**. (After the revolution of 1905 a small group of SRs adopted the name **SR Maximalists** and this group retained a shadowy existence during the years 1917-21.)

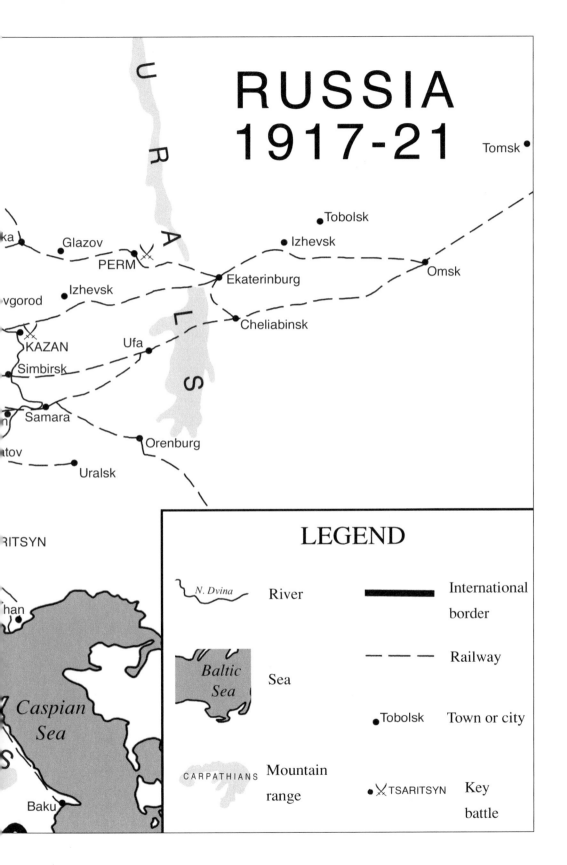

RUSSIA 1917-21

Tomsk •

• Tobolsk

• Izhevsk

ka •

Glazov •

PERM ✕✕

Ekaterinburg •

Omsk •

Izhevsk •

vgorod •

Cheliabinsk •

✕✕
KAZAN

Ufa •

Simbirsk

Samara •

Orenburg •

atov •

Uralsk •

RITSYN

han •

Caspian
Sea

Baku •

LEGEND

~N. Dvina~   River

Baltic
Sea   Sea

CARPATHIANS   Mountain
range

▬▬▬▬▬   International
border

– – – –   Railway

• Tobolsk   Town or city

• ✕ TSARITSYN   Key
battle

Introduction

*It must never be forgotten that in the Russian
revolutionary wars there were* three *parties in
the struggle – the Reds, the 'Whites', and the
People – and that, as much as the populace
detested the Red regime in its earliest form, they
came, during the revolutionary wars, to regard
the 'Whites' with even greater repugnance.*
Sir Paul Dukes
Secret Agent 'ST 25'

Any account of Russia's civil war published in the twenty-first century has to
take account of the very obvious fact that the state created by the Bolsheviks
between 1917 and 1921 collapsed in the autumn of 1991. In the thoughtful
conclusion to her overview of Soviet foreign policy in the twentieth century
Caroline Kennedy-Pike noted:

> Perhaps the greatest paradox in this tale about the Soviet
> experience and the outside world was that the propagation of a
> radial new economic and political global system was based on a
> remarkably fragile political and economic system at home.

The origin of that fragility Kennedy-Pike located in the civil war, which
'showed that the Soviet regime was at the very least a contested one right from
its inception'.[1] It is the contested origins of the Soviet state which this short
account of Russia's civil war seeks to explore. It will help explain why, even in
its heyday as a world superpower, the Soviet regime was never more than
sullenly accepted by the Soviet people.

Traditionally histories of the civil war have concentrated on the struggle
between the Bolsheviks, the Reds, and the Whites, led by Admiral Kolchak in
the East, General Denikin in the South and General Yudenich in the West.
From this perspective it was always a war between good and evil – usually the
Reds representing progress and the Whites reaction, although sometimes these
roles were reversed. This perspective was fine when the Soviet Union existed
as an apparently stable state. Approached in this way the civil war was all about
establishing the legitimacy of the Soviet Union, and broad generalizations

about progress and reaction were enough. The problem with such an approach from the perspective of the twenty-first Century is that the Red versus White struggle gives no basis from which to understand the emergence of the Soviet Union as a 'fragile' state. The vast majority of the Russian population were united in their opposition to the forces represented by the White Generals. Those social groups represented in the White armies fared badly in the Constituent Assembly elections of November 1917; the non-socialist parties won just under eight per cent of the vote.[2] Then, during the civil war itself, the Whites made clear they were unembarrassed by the symbols of the Tsarist past and made no attempt to address the social ills which had led to the collapse of the *ancien régime*; they had no labour programme and no land policy worthy of the name. The defeat of the Whites could not have traumatized soviet society to such an extent that it remained forever 'fragile'.

If the Red versus White struggle cannot satisfactorily explain the concept of 'fragility' where can it be found? The answer comes from Russia's other civil war, the struggle which twenty five years ago the historian Oliver Radkey characterized as Russia's 'unknown civil war', the war between the Reds and Russia's peasant armies, or Greens.[3] The Russian civil war was a three-cornered fight, not a simple clash between two opposing sides. This was clear at the time to those able to observe the struggle at close quarters. Sir Paul Dukes, Britain's master spy in 1919, resident in Petrograd throughout that year, summed up the war in the epigram which opens this Introduction. Yet even those whose knowledge of the civil war is limited to the film of Boris Pasternak's classic novel *Doctor Zhivago* will remember how the hero ends up joining a group of partisans based in Siberia. These were the Greens. The Greens fought in the interests of the peasants. Sometimes their leaders were anarchists, more usually members of the Socialist Revolutionary Party (SRs), but as the historian Peter Kenez pointed out a quarter of a century ago, whether anarchist or SR led, the movements were strikingly similar.[4] In the Constituent Assembly elections of November 1917 the SRs won fifty-five per cent of the vote.[5] By April 1921 165 large peasant insurgent detachments were active in Russia, of which 140 (numbering 118,000) were associated with the SR Party.[6] The front cover of this volume shows the Red Army advancing across the frozen Gulf of Finland to crush the most famous Green insurgency of this time, the March 1921 anarchist-led Kronstadt rebellion. The Bolsheviks' war against the Greens, their war against their own people, was the ultimate source of the Soviet Union's 'fragility'.

The Greens are, of course, acknowledged in every account of the civil war. Similarly, every study of the civil war notes that the fighting began with a confusing 'democratic phase' which occurred during the summer of 1918. Before the White Generals came on the scene in late autumn 1918 the competing sides were the Moscow-based Bolsheviks and the SRs, who, supported by the rather mysterious Czechoslovak Legion, established on the Volga a government responsible to the Constituent Assembly elected in

November 1917 which the Bolsheviks had forcibly dispersed. However, this episode, like Radkey's 'unknown' civil war of 1921, is traditionally treated as a distraction from the main story of how the Reds overcame the Whites. What is different about this short history is that it will show how there is a clear continuity between that first democratic phase of the civil war in summer 1918 and the 'unknown' peasant wars of early 1921. Moreover, this book will argue that Russia's civil war did not only begin and end with a clash between the Bolsheviks and the peasantry, but that this struggle was continuous and that it complicated, indeed almost wrecked, the Red struggle against the Whites.

In my *Origins of the Russian Civil War* I tried to retrieve from Trotsky's dustbin of history those first few months of the civil war in summer 1918, when the White Generals played no significant part and the civil war was a struggle between the urban-based Bolsheviks, who in October 1917 had won a majority on the All-Russian Soviet of Workers and Soldiers' Deputies, and the village-based SR Party, which in November 1917 had won the elections to the Constituent Assembly. Controversially, I suggested then, and repeat here, that this was a struggle which the SRs nearly won. The administrations the SRs established, first on the Volga – Komuch (The Committee of the Constituent Assembly) – then in Omsk – the Directory – have been pilloried in the memoirs of both Reds and Whites as ineffectual; actually they put down deep popular roots. As will be shown below, members of Komuch turned up as Green leaders on the Black Sea coast in late 1919, while the symbols of that administration would become the emblems of most bands of Siberian Greens.

In order to give added stress to the continuity between the first democratic phase of the civil war and the later clashes between the Bolsheviks and the peasantry I have deliberately used the description Green anachronistically. It was a term current in the years 1919 to 1921 which was not used in 1918; then the SRs simply described themselves as democratic socialists and to the confusion of many foreign observers continued to display the red flag; it was only in 1919 that green hat bands began to appear. However, the continuities between summer 1918 and the rest of the civil war are real. Those who by the end of the civil war were described as Greens had begun the civil war as democratic socialists, and so, to dramatize the tripartite nature of the struggle, I have used the shorthand of Reds, Whites and Greens throughout.

If the Red versus White struggle cannot explain the 'fragility' of the soviet regime, the Red versus Green civil war certainly can. In her 1996 study of peasant attitudes in 1930 the historian Lyn Viola has shown how stubbornly the peasants resisted Stalin's collectivization campaign. She described how 'peasants banded together in self-defence as a cultural community struggling for survival in the face of the state's frontal assault on the household economy, peasant customs, and ways of living'.[7] It had been the same a decade earlier. This book will highlight the extent of peasant resistance to the first collectivization measures of 1919. The approach adopted in this volume is therefore rather similar to that of Andrea Graziosi's seminal essay describing the whole period 1917 – 1933 as the 'great soviet peasant war'.[8] With Graziosi it will be suggested that in 1921 the Red versus Green civil war ended in a rather unsatisfactory stalemate. The Bolsheviks were forced to make economic concessions to the peasants, but reserved the right to resume the struggle once they had caught their breath. If Russia's civil war of 1917 – 1921 is seen as part of a broader civil conflict which only ended in the early 1930s, the 'fragility' of the Soviet Union as a state never at ease with itself begins to be understood.

The horrors of the Stalinist years began in the civil war. Like all civil wars Russia's civil war was a social conflict which spilled over into armed struggle. It was, therefore, a war characterized as much by bestial massacres as military struggle, and the concentration in this volume on political and social issues is inevitable; the fighting often seemed incidental to the struggle more broadly defined. The first historian of the struggle, N.E. Kakurin, calculated that although the military casualties of the fighting were two to two and a half times less than those suffered by Russia in the First World War, the civilian casualties were two or even three times greater, a stark statistic speaking volumes for the nature of the war and its impact on society.[9] According to Britain's leading student of the fighting, the war resulted in 1,287,000 deaths from battle or disease in the opposing armies and nearer 1,500,000 if deaths through execution are added.[10]

The events described in the chapters which follow tell a complex story, but the underlying message is a relatively simple one which follows Sir Paul Dukes's pithy summary: the Reds could not win alone. When the Bolsheviks, the Reds, tried to take on both the People, the Greens, and the Whites, they risked annihilation. When the Bolsheviks had an understanding, however tenuous, with representatives of Green groups, they could contain the Whites with ease. It was, therefore, only after the Reds and the Greens had together defeated the Whites that the Red versus Green struggle could finally be resolved – and when it was, it resulted not in victory but in stalemate.

Recent Accounts

In western scholarship the definitive study of the civil war has been for many years now Evan Mawdsley's *The Russian Civil War*. It is referred to often in this account and is still an essential text especially in terms of battles fought and foreign aid received. What has changed since its publication in 1987 is a growing interest in, and the possibility of researching into, the social aspects of the civil war. This approach was first adopted, as far as the southern front was concerned, by Peter Kenez a decade before Mawdsley's study, but it was only in the 1990s that similar work was done on other aspects of the fighting. The social history of the Siberian front has been explored by two scholars: N.G.O. Pereira's *White Siberia: The Politics of Civil War* is particularly strong on the partisan movement in Siberia, while Jonathan Smele's *Civil War in Siberia* is the definitive history of Admiral Kolchak and his regime. As to the Bolshevik regime, Vladimir Brovkin's *Behind the Front Lines of the Civil War* gives a detailed picture of the political struggles and social upheavals which disrupted the Bolsheviks' war effort.

Some of the most interesting work of the last decade has been written about the Don front, partly inspired by the enduring popularity of Mikhail Sholokhov's epic novel *The Quiet Don*. Brian Murphy published the first full account of the Don rebellion of March 1919 in the journal *Revolutionary Russia*, and his *The Russian Civil War: Primary Sources* reproduces in English translation a number of documents never previously published, some of the most interesting of which refer to the career of the Bolshevik cavalry commander S.M. Budyenny. Murphy's publications complement the massive Russian language document collection devoted to the career of the Don Cossack Filip Mironov, *Filip Mironov: Tikhii Don v 1917 – 1921 gg.*. The Bolsheviks' decision to execute this radical SR, who had always fought against the Whites is a dramatic example of the Soviet Union's original sin, which condemned it to ultimate collapse.

As the Mironov and Murphy collections highlight, the disintegration of the Soviet Union was associated with the opening of long closed archives. A selection of documents from these was brought together by the late Vladimir Petrovich Butt, who at the time the Soviet Union collapsed was trying to gather material for the Soviet Academy of Science's long planned official history of the civil war, and published as *The Russian Civil War: Documents from the Soviet Archives*. A new generation of Russian scholars has been particularly active in the archives and has published in Russian academic journals a number of studies of 'Green' unrest, a theme which is also taken up by some of the contributors to Brovkin's *The Bolsheviks in Russian Society*.[11]

Before the Fighting Started

Russia's civil war began when political groups of both Left and Right, frustrated by the way Russia's democracy was developing after the Tsar's overthrow in February 1917, decided to take up arms against it. The first to move were the Whites. Restorationist or White forces did not necessarily want to restore the Tsar to the throne, but they did want to replace Russia's rather chaotic post February 1917 democracy, which they saw as chaos pure and simple, with an authoritarian regime which would defend their privileges. The origins of the Whites' civil war were in events which took place less than two months after Tsar Nicholas II had been overthrown and a new Provisional Government established. At the end of April 1917 conservative elements in the army, linked to leading industrialists, began to plan a coup. They were stung into action by the political crisis of April 1917 which epitomized for them the chaos they feared so much. This April Crisis, the first serious crisis experienced by the new Provisional Government, was essentially a clash between the rival authorities claimed by the Provisional Government itself and the Petrograd Soviet (Council) of Workers' and Soldiers' Deputies. The first Provisional Government established after the overthrow of the Tsar was dominated by liberal politicians; the moderate socialists – the Menshevik Social Democrats and the SRs – initially had preferred to keep their distance from the government and build up a power base in the Petrograd Soviet of Workers' and Soldiers' Deputies.

On 20 and 21 April the Provisional Government clashed with the Petrograd Soviet on the question of peace, or rather peace terms. In 1917 the First World War was still raging on the Western Front and Russia's new Provisional Government had made clear it was determined to remain in the war and keep open the Eastern Front. The Soviet was happy enough to support the war effort, but wanted to be clear as to why they were fighting and, therefore, what were the war aims and potential peace terms for any settlement. For the Soviet an issue of principle was at stake. If Russia was to continue playing its part with Britain and France in the First World War, it had to be as a democratic government working for the earliest possible peace; the Soviet had promised to support the Provisional Government so long as it worked for peace 'without annexations or indemnities'. However, despite this clear pronouncement from the Soviet the Provisional Government's liberal Foreign Minister had informed Britain and France that Russia still stood by the previous treaties signed by the Tsar, which envisaged Russian expansion after the war into the Dardanelles.

When this news leaked out, the Soviet was furious and a series of protest demonstrations were organized during which shots were fired. The Provisional Government was uncertain how to respond. The Commander of the Petrograd Military District, General Lavr Kornilov, prepared to restore order in the way military men often prefer, by opening fire on the demonstrators. Government ministers were not so sure. Quite by chance, the Provisional Government discussed General Kornilov's request to open fire on the demonstrators in the presence of Admiral A.V. Kolchak, who happened to be in Petrograd at the time on unrelated business. Kolchak, who would play such a crucial role in Russia's civil war – and who was at this time Admiral of the Black Sea Fleet – therefore witnessed at first hand how, in a verbal duel between Kornilov and the then Minister of Justice Alexander Kerensky, Kornilov was forced to back down. Kerensky, who was at this time the only socialist in the first Provisional Government, was the leading parliamentary spokesman of the SR Party and the man who would soon become first Minister of War and then Prime Minister.[12]

Having decided not to confront the Soviet by opening fire on the demonstrators, the Provisional Government had no choice but to come to terms with its representatives. The April political crisis was resolved without recourse to the use of force, but, from the perspective of Kornilov and Kolchak, only at the cost of bringing representatives of the Soviet into the Provisional

Government. After the April crisis the Provisional Government was reformed as the First Coalition Government a coalition of liberals, Mensheviks, and SRs. Agreed on the need to continue Russia's part in the First World War, but divided on all issues of social reform, the First Coalition Government epitomized 'weak' government. Not surprisingly disappointed politicians on the restorationist Right saw it taking Russia further down the road to chaos. The Right looked to both Kornilov and Kolchak as potential leaders, for both had at least tried to stand up to those 'soft' on the Soviet during the April crisis. Within days of the formation of the First Coalition Government a shadowy organization known as the Society for the Economic Rehabilitation of Russia had been formed by leading industrialists and had established contact with Kornilov's adjutant.

Little came of these early counter-revolutionary plans, largely because Kornilov was transferred to the South West Front in preparation for the offensive which the new coalition government planned to launch in June against German and Austrian forces. The Society for the Economic Rehabilitation of Russia, however, did not give up its plotting. Kolchak resigned his post as Admiral of the Black Sea Fleet in protest at the new government's decision to appoint Kerensky as Minister of War; he was, therefore, kicking his heals in Petrograd from early June until 20 July awaiting a new posting. At once Kolchak rather than Kornilov became the focus for a right-wing press campaign, funded by the Society for the Economic Rehabilitation of Russia, which called for Kolchak's appointment as an emergency 'strong' prime minister in Russia's hour of crisis. This campaign reached its height when the military offensive launched on the Eastern Front on 18 June rapidly turned to a rout and the First Coalition Government fell apart.[13]

As the restorationist Right clamoured for Kolchak, the Bolshevik Left began to mobilize. Ever since early June 1917 the Bolsheviks had been talking about staging an insurrection to bring down the coalition government; the political crisis brought about by the failure of the June offensive seemed to offer the perfect opportunity. The first moves were made as the First All-Russian Congress of Soviets of Workers' and Soldiers' Deputies met in Petrograd from 3-24 June. The Bolsheviks drew up plans for a demonstration to be held on 10 June which would pressurize the Congress of Soviets to denounce the First Coalition Government and take power into its own hands. However, when the Congress of Soviets made clear it would ban the Bolsheviks' demonstration, they backed down. This was a tactical retreat. The Bolsheviks were buoyed up by the amount of support they received a week later in a Soviet sponsored demonstration, and very aware of the growing anger among many army garrison units as orders came through to transfer soldiers from Petrograd to the front as the offensive got under way.

The First Machine Gun Regiment had already decided to take some form of action when news came through on 2 July that the First Coalition Government had collapsed. With the Machine Gunners quite capable of seizing the city, and the government in disarray, the moment for an uprising seemed to have come. Some in the Bolshevik leadership were concerned that the revolutionary mood in Petrograd was not matched throughout the country, but rank and file pressure overcame that caution. By the evening of 3 July Machine Gunners manned road blocks throughout the city and the following day armed demonstrators marched to the Soviet building calling for a new soviet government. Things, it seemed, could go either way. One moment Lenin was discussing possible cabinet portfolios within a new Bolshevik administration, the next it had become all too clear that loyal troops were approaching the city and the Bolsheviks would have to back down. By the evening of 4 July it was all over.[14]

So by early July 1917 the three sides in Russia's civil war were already crystallizing. Dreams of a White counter-revolution were already well advanced among the supporters of Kornilov, Kolchak and the Society for the Economic Rehabilitation of Russia. Although the Bolshevik Party leadership was far from united on the policy of insurrection, a majority of party activists had welcomed the preparations for the armed coup in July. And in the middle stood Russia's democratic majority, now headed by Kerensky. He resolved the government crisis of July 1917 by working to establish a Second Coalition Government supported by liberals, Mensheviks and SRs. Kerensky became its Prime Minister.

ONE

Red Defeat?

In summer 1917 the fledgling democracy established in Russia after the February overthrow of the Tsar found itself under threat from two sides, the 'White' restorationist Right, who wanted to turn the clock of History backwards, and the 'Red' Bolshevik Left, who wanted to advance the clock of History and turn Russia's democratic revolution into the world's first socialist revolution. Although it would be 1918 before either of these threats resulted in widespread fighting, Russia's civil war started with coup attempts by both Whites and Reds, executed in the late summer and autumn of 1917, but planned much earlier. On 27 August 1917 the Russian Army Supreme Commander General Lavr Kornilov tried to stage a coup and impose a new administration which would restore to influence the political and social elites so recently overthrown by the people of Russia. He failed. Then, on 24 October 1917, the Bolshevik Party succeeded in staging a coup, but a coup which was only partially successful. The Bolsheviks seized power and announced the formation of their own government; but, under popular pressure, they backed down. They formed instead a coalition administration with radical SRs, a genuine soviet government, since it comprised the party which had a majority in the workers' and soldiers' soviet, the Bolsheviks, and the party which had a majority in the peasants' soviet, the Left SRs. While this coalition administration remained in tact the threat of civil war remained just a threat.

Although it flickered in autumn 1917, the civil war proper was ignited by Lenin's twin decisions in spring 1918 to sign a peace treaty with Germany and to start the construction of a socialist state by socializing Russia's agriculture. No SR, moderate or radical, could accept such policies. By May 1918 the Bolsheviks were determined to press ahead with the establishment of a single party dictatorship, and the SRs were determined to stop them. By June 1918 SR insurrections on the Volga had resulted in the formation of a rival democratic government and the 'Red versus Green' civil war had begun. Russia's Green forces were not defeated militarily in this first phase of the fighting. Initially they were very successful, and their capture of Kazan in August 1918 created panic among the Bolshevik leadership. Thereafter the Bolsheviks' Red Army counter-attacked, and the Green 'People's Army' was forced to retreat. That retreat ended in October 1918, and by the end of the month it was the People's Army which was advancing. The Reds were retreating when Kolchak and his White forces staged a coup, arrested Russia's democratic government, and turned a Red-Green civil war into a Red-White civil war.

White Coup

Preparations for a White coup began in earnest after General Kornilov had been made Supreme Commander-in-Chief of Russia's Armed Forces on 18 July 1917. This appointment requires some contextualization, since it was strange for Russia's new Prime Minister, Kerensky, to appoint to such an important post someone with whom he had already clashed in April. Kerensky, appointed Prime Minister after the collapse of the First Coalition Government, was committed to the principle of a cross-class coalition administration. He had little difficulty persuading the Mensheviks and SRs to serve under him, but he had to buy the support of the liberals by appointing Commander-in-Chief someone with a reputation which might restore the Army's battered morale. Kornilov was the obvious choice, but he was still in contact with the Society for the Economic Rehabilitation of Russia, the group of right-wing politicians and industrialists who had been plotting a coup since April. Kerensky hoped to counter this danger by making himself Minister of War and appointing leading SRs as Deputy Minister of War and Navy Minister: the former terrorist Boris Savinkov was Deputy Minister of War and V.I. Lebedev Navy Minister.

Once Kornilov had been appointed Commander-in-Chief, counter-revolutionary plotting began in earnest. One of the earliest military figures to be brought into the affair was General A.I. Denikin, Commander of the South-west Front, but many of the key conspirators continued to be the industrialists associated with the Society for the Economic Rehabilitation of Russia. Leading members of Russia's old social elite gathered in Moscow on 8-10 August to attend the so-called Meeting of Civic Figures. In public this assembly discussed plans for the agenda of the forthcoming Moscow State Conference, a gathering summoned by the Second Coalition Government in an attempt to gauge the political mood of the nation; it met in Moscow from 13-14 August. In private, however, delegates to the Meeting of Civil Figures plotted counter-revolution with emissaries sent by General Kornilov. Kornilov's rapturous reception by right-wing delegates to the Moscow State Conference only strengthened the determination of the plotters to act. Kornilov anticipated that the Petrograd Soviet would organize demonstrations at the end of August to commemorate six months since the overthrow of the Tsar; according to his plan, the army would brand these demonstrations as mutinous, dissolve the Soviet and take power. Kornilov was optimistic that he might be able to persuade some of the current government ministers, in particular Kerensky and Savinkov, to support his action. However he made very clear to his closest supporters that if Kerensky and Savinkov refused to sanction his initiative, he would act alone.

Kerensky, aware that the Bolsheviks were recovering from their July fiasco, was also worried about the possibility of a clash with the Soviet in the event of demonstrations at the end of August. So, on 23 August, he sent Savinkov to hold talks with Kornilov. On the question of possible demonstrations, the two men soon agreed that no such demonstrations should be allowed and a force of Cossacks led by General P.N. Krasnov should be readied to disperse them. They also agreed that if force were used to disperse the demonstrations, some sort of government reshuffle might follow in order to bring into the ruling coalition more ministers known for their pro-war views. Understandably, in view of this conversation with Savinkov, Kornilov began the final stage of his preparations convinced that Kerensky and Savinkov would endorse his action and be rewarded with seats in the post-coup government.

Kornilov's coup foundered when Kerensky realized that Kornilov wanted to replace him as Prime Minister. Kerensky did not want a seat in a right-wing government headed by Kornilov. He wanted to remain prime minister of a coalition government, even if after an armed clash with Soviet demonstrators it was one which had moved to a more pronounced pro-war and therefore right-wing stance: if there were a clash with the Soviet and force had to be used, Kornilov could execute that force; but it was never Kerensky's idea that, whatever other posts might be reshuffled, he would resign and Kornilov would take his place. In the dramatic exchange of views between the two men on 26 August (an exchange which took place using the Hughes apparatus, a primitive form of teleprinter) it quickly emerged that the two men were at cross purposes. Kornilov freely admitted he wanted to use a clash with the Soviet to change the government, for he and Savinkov had both agreed that this was necessary. Kornilov assumed that Kerensky and Savinkov meant the same as him by the term 'changing the government', but clearly they did not. When Kerensky realized Kornilov intended to replace him, not just to serve as his strong man, Kerensky accused Kornilov of treason and called on the Soviet to resist the coup attempt. When Krasnov's Cossacks sent to take control of Petrograd realized they would be opposed by forces rapidly mobilized by the Soviet they declined to act. Within hours Kornilov had been arrested and his coup attempt had ended in abject failure. The White plots had got nowhere.[1]

Red Coup

The attempted coup by Kornilov radicalized Russian society. The liberals, many of whom had been closely identified with Kornilov, were seen by a majority in the Soviet to have lost the right to participate in any future democratic government. As Kerensky strove to create a Third Coalition Government which would include those liberals not tainted by too close an association with Kornilov, pressure grew from within the soviets for a 'soviet government', a government formed by the socialist parties represented in the soviet, a socialist coalition without liberals. In the heady atmosphere after Kornilov's defeat, the Soviet decided to be more pro-active. It had organized the mass popular protest action which prevented Kornilov seizing power, it would now try to help establish a new democratic government. It would organize a Democratic Conference to be attended by local soviets, trade unions and cooperatives; a body which would act as a counterweight to the Moscow State Conference which had proved such a focal point for Kornilov and his restorationists. In the crisis of Kornilov's coup attempt, the Second Coalition Government had collapsed and the demand for a government made up exclusively from the socialist parties represented in the soviet, a soviet government, was increasingly popular. The demand for a 'Soviet Government' was put to the Democratic Conference, when it opened on 14 September, by the leader of the Bolshevik delegation, L.B. Kamenev. In a complex series of votes and backstage deals this proposal was first supported and then rejected. Kerensky eventually got his way and a Third Coalition Government was formed to hold power until elections were held to a Constituent Assembly in November. However, he could not ignore the pressure for a Soviet government. The attraction of a Soviet government was that it would at least be responsible to some sort of democratically representative body, the soviets, until elections could be held to a Constituent Assembly. To provide an alternative focus of democratic responsibility Kerensky's government promised it would establish an interim constitutional body of its own called the Preparliament.

The formation of the Third Coalition Government and the associated Preparliament caused division in all political parties. However, the divisions caused in Kerensky's own party, the SR Party, condemned the Preparliament experiment to failure. Back in April 1917 the SR Party's pro-war faction had launched its own newspaper *Volya naroda* as a rival to the official party paper *Delo naroda*. On its editorial board were V.I. Lebedev, the future Navy Minister, and P.A. Sorokin, who would play a prominent part in the first phase of the civil war. This powerful grouping backed Kerensky fully. However, when on 24 September the SR Party Central Committee voted to support the Third Coalition Government, the party leader V.M. Chernov refused to attend any more Central Committee meetings in protest and announced that he would boycott the Preparliament. Chernov was not alone. He stood at the centre of the SR Party. Those radicals to his left were even more impatient with the party's support for Kerensky and his determination to continue an alliance with the liberals. During the Democratic Conference these left-wing members of the SR Party refused to cooperate with those on the right who supported Kerensky's government and were well on the way to forming a separate political party. Within days of opening on 7 October, under the chairmanship of the Right SR and former Minister of the Interior N.D.

Avksentiev, the Preparliament faced a crisis. The veteran socialist N.V. Chaikovskii, whose revolutionary career had begun in the 1870s and who in 1917 led Russia's cooperative societies as a member of the moderate Popular Socialist Party, worked hard to assemble a pro-Kerensky majority within the Preparliament, but the government programme he advanced was rejected. The Preparliament's debate on the state of the army was equally disastrous; initiated on 10 October, it ended on 19 October when the Minister of War resigned after a disagreement with the Minister of Foreign Affairs.

Kerensky's Third Coalition Government finally foundered on 24 October. Since 6 October the Commander of the Petrograd Military District had been under orders to prepare the troops of the Petrograd garrison for transfer to the front, since a German attack seemed imminent. The soldiers concerned reacted with fury and, to prevent this transfer happening, the Petrograd Soviet established a Military Revolutionary Committee (MRC) on 16 October. By 21 October Kerensky and the MRC were at loggerheads and the MRC informed the Petrograd Military District that henceforth soldiers would not obey orders unless countersigned by the MRC; to ensure this happened the MRC would appoint its own commissars to military units. When these commissars were in place, on 23 October, the MRC announced that it had the right to veto all military orders. Faced on 24 October with what seemed to be a mutiny, Kerensky tried to initiate criminal proceedings against the MRC and moved to close down the Bolshevik newspapers responsible for encouraging the activities of the MRC and its commissars. Yet when the Preparliament debated Kerensky's actions, it took the side of the MRC and passed a vote of no confidence in him. The Preparliament declined to support Kerensky in his confrontation with the Petrograd Soviet, and at the same time passed a resolution calling for land to be distributed to the peasants and peace talks to begin at once in consultation with the Allies.[2]

With the Third Coalition Government visibly crumbling, it was obvious to the Bolsheviks that the slogan a 'Soviet Government' was increasingly popular. The issue at stake was how best to implement that slogan. The formation of the Preparliament had not only caused division within the SR Party but also among the Bolsheviks. Since the Kornilov rebellion the Petrograd Soviet had had a Bolshevik majority and the leader of the Bolsheviks there, Kamenev, argued for a parliamentary road to power. Kerensky's hold over the Preparliament was shaky: the Bolsheviks, therefore, should work in the Preparliament, undermine support for Kerensky, and win popular endorsement for the idea of a Soviet Government, as first proposed at the Democratic Conference. There was much talk of expelling the liberal representatives of the propertied classes from the Preparliament and transforming it into a Revolutionary Convention which would rule until the Constituent Assembly was elected.

Lenin saw things very differently. Since Kerensky had become Prime Minister in July, Lenin had been forced into hiding as an alleged German agent responsible for the anti-war demonstrations which had brought down the First Coalition Government. In hiding he had reread Marx's writings on the Paris Commune of 1871 and had convinced himself that, in the changed situation of Russia in 1917, a 'Petrograd Commune' could succeed, since it would not be isolated in the way the Paris Commune had been; a commune in Petrograd would be the signal for a revolution not only in Russia but for associated revolutions throughout Europe. Kamenev, obsessed with political manoeuvring in the Petrograd Soviet and the Democratic Conference, and anticipating doing the same in the Preparliament, had, Lenin believed, lost his sense of History. Kamenev could not see the wood for the trees. There was a chance that the Bolsheviks, acting as the agents of History itself, could establish the first ever Marxist state and start a world revolution. This belief convinced Lenin of the need to ditch democracy. Working, as Kamenev was, to break up Kerensky's coalition and replace it with a democratic coalition of socialist parties would not address the agenda of world socialism; it could only address the more mundane issues of peace and land.

Lenin was therefore determined that the Bolshevik Party should boycott the Preparliament and prepare to seize power. From mid-September his constant refrain from his exile in Finland was that the time for insurrection had come and that a peaceful resolution of the crisis, as proposed by Kamenev, was impossible. He recognized that insurrection meant launching 'a civil war in its highest and most decisive form', but saw no harm to the revolution stemming from this. Initially Lenin's views were ignored by the rest of the Central Committee. The party entered the Preparliament and began talks about forming 'a ministry of similar parties'; it took Lenin's threat of resignation to convince the Central Committee that the Bolsheviks should walk out of the Preparliament. Thereafter, on 10 October, the party voted for the principle of insurrection. Yet even then this was at first a statement of intent rather than a guide to action. Little was done in a practical sense to prepare for an insurrection until the clash developed between Kerensky and the MRC. As that dispute became more intense, and Kerensky prepared to move against the MRC and the Bolshevik press, the Bolshevik Party was goaded by Lenin first to respond and then to take the initiative.

On the evening of 24 October Lenin arrived in Petrograd, urging the party to take advantage of their confrontation with Kerensky. They may have stumbled towards insurrection, he said, but they should now act:

> Everything now hangs by a thread; we are confronted by problems which are not to be solved by conferences or congresses.... We must at all costs, this very evening, this very night, arrest the government... We must not wait! We may lose everything![3]

Thus, as delegates gathered for the Second All-Russian Congress of Soviets on 25 October they learned that Lenin and the Bolsheviks had seized power

Bolshevik soldiers assembling in Moscow.

during the night and established a Bolshevik Government. Given the Preparliament's vote of no confidence in Kerensky's government earlier on the 24th, the delegates had always assumed that they would debate the formation of a 'Soviet Government', but a soviet government which would take the form of a coalition administration of all the parties represented in the soviet. To be told by Lenin that the Bolsheviks had formed such a government alone, without the inclusion of any coalition partners and without the need for any democratic debate, came as a considerable surprise. For Lenin, by this action, had seized power not on behalf of the soviet, as he claimed, but from the other democratic parties represented in Russia's soviets, notably the 'Green' SRs.

Civil War Confined

Lenin had called for an insurrection in the full knowledge that it might lead to civil war. Kerensky, who slipped away from Petrograd before he could be arrested by the Bolsheviks, succeeded in rallying some Cossack troops loyal to General Krasnov and with these he planned to march on Petrograd. At the same time those SRs loyal to Kerensky's Third Coalition Government formed a Committee for the Salvation of the Revolution and the Motherland, which hoped to stage a counter-insurrection against the Bolsheviks as Kerensky marched on Petrograd. In order to stop this nascent Red-Green civil war the Railway Workers' Union delegation to the Second Congress of Soviets declared on 26 October that it would stop all movement on the railways until talks had been held on the formation of a coalition socialist administration responsible to the soviets, in other words a genuinely soviet government. These talks began on 28 October and had an immediate impact. The majority of the Committee for the Salvation of the Revolution and the Motherland, including its SR leader V.M. Zenzinov, came out against Kerensky's threat of force and agreed to support a negotiated settlement. At the same time Zenzinov's committee distanced itself from the small group of liberals who encouraged officer cadets to take up arms against the Bolsheviks in the early hours of 29 October in a futile attempt to dislodge Lenin's government.

As to the Bolsheviks, Kamenev was also more than willing to respond to the Railway Workers' Union initiative and seek a compromise. He stressed that what the country needed was the sort of all-socialist coalition government the Bolsheviks had proposed at the Democratic Conference; such an administration could hold the ring until the elections to the Constituent Assembly had been held. As the talks engineered by the Railway Workers' Union developed, the SRs dropped their insistence that the Bolsheviks could not be included in any government, and the Bolsheviks dropped their insistence that Lenin and Trotsky had to be offered ministerial posts. After many hours of negotiation it was also agreed that the planned coalition socialist administration would be responsible to an expanded Soviet until the Constituent Assembly met. With progress towards a compromise so well advanced, there was little will to fight. Kerensky and Krasnov's forces arrived at Pulkovo Heights outside Petrograd (today the site of the airport) on 30 October. There they confronted a hastily gathered Red force. That force was led not by a Bolshevik but by the radical SR Colonel M.A. Muraviev, who was convinced that the formation of a genuine soviet government was imminent. The Cossack commander Krasnov had hoped that one cavalry charge would suffice to terrorize the lightly armed Red Guards; but under Muraviev's guidance they stood firm. When it was clear that there would be bitter fighting, the Cossacks announced that they too supported a genuine soviet government, a negotiated settlement as being proposed by the Railway Worker's Union.

Lenin had been prepared to let Kamenev take the lead in the talks organized by the Railway Workers' Union while there was a real danger that Kerensky might retake power. When Krasnov's Cossacks began to return peaceably to their homes on the river Don, Lenin restated his determination to form an exclusively Bolshevik government. As Lenin and Kamenev vied for influence, the Bolshevik Central Committee voted first, on 31 October, to support the idea of a socialist coalition, then, on 1 November, accepted Lenin's amendment that they should do so only to play for time, and subsequently, later on the 1st, voted once again for Kamenev's proposal. Lenin countered on

2 November, when he again persuaded the Central Committee to back a purely Bolshevik government, but this decision was not endorsed by the Bolshevik delegation to the Soviet, which continued to back Kamenev. Finally, on 3 November, when the Railway Workers' Union talks were due to endorse the planned agreement, Lenin got the Central Committee to send Joseph Stalin to attend the meeting in the place of Kamenev. Stalin, as he had been ordered, wrecked the agreement and as a consequence Kamenev and his supporters resigned from both the Central Committee and Lenin's government on 4 November.[4]

Ten days after the Bolshevik seizure of power, the Bolshevik Party was in disarray. To avoid a Red-Green civil war Kamenev had insisted that the Bolsheviks should not rule alone and in the end his resignation worked. In the crisis which followed the resignations the forces of compromise gained the upper hand. Hopes for some sort of coalition socialist administration were strengthened when the Extraordinary Congress of Peasant Soviets was held in Petrograd on 10 November. Muraviev had not been the only radical SR to decide he had more in common with the Bolsheviks than Kerensky. During the Railway Workers' Union talks the left wing of the SR Party had formally constituted themselves as a separate political party, and these Left SRs won a majority at the Extraordinary Congress of Peasant Soviets. The Left SRs endorsed the call of the Railway Workers' Union for a coalition socialist administration, and began drafting plans for some form of merger between the Soviet, which represented only workers and soldiers, and the Peasants' Soviet. When the Second Congress of Peasants' Soviets endorsed this arrangement on 27 November, the Left SRs joined Lenin's government taking up their posts on 8 December.[5] The successful formation of this coalition socialist administration, rather than Lenin's initial preference for a purely socialist administration, had enormous significance. At the most basic level it ended at once any prospect of a renewal of fighting between the Bolsheviks and the SRs, the sort of Red-Green struggle which had nearly developed at Pulkovo Heights. Kerensky and the Right SRs, for all their disagreements with their Left SR former comrades, were not going to take up arms against them.

This was made clear by the SR Party's initial response to the results of the Constituent Assembly elections held in mid-November. Although the elections were won by the SRs, it was not a straight-forward victory. They had won 55 per cent of the seats but this figure included the Ukrainian SR Party, which was formally independent and politically well to the left of the national party leadership, while many of the key SR organizations in Petrograd, on the Volga, and among the sailors of the Baltic Fleet, were by autumn 1917 in the hands of the Left SRs. Both the Bolsheviks and the Left SRs canvassed the notion that the Soviets and the Constituent Assembly could merge to form some sort of 'Revolutionary Convention'. Timetables were adjusted so that the Constituent Assembly, the Third Congress of Soviets and the Third Congress of Peasants' Soviets would all meet in early January 1918 so as to make just such a merger possible. The idea was dropped when the majority of Constituent Assembly delegates refused to go along with the idea.[6]

The response of the Bolshevik-Left SR coalition administration was to dissolve the Constituent Assembly; but even then the response of other SRs was muted. They protested but they did not respond with talk of an immediate insurrection. On the contrary, they were prepared to work within the new soviet democratic framework, established by the Third Congress of Soviets in January 1918. This was in line with a policy agreed six weeks earlier. Although the right-wing SRs appeared to have the initiative on 22 November 1917 when the SR group of deputies to the Constituent Assembly set up a special Committee to Defend the Constituent Assembly under the leadership of Chaikovskii – and stirring speeches were made by the likes of Zenzinov, Sorokin and their colleague Ya.T. Dedusenko – the Fourth Congress of the SR Party met from 26 November to 5 December and was a triumph for Chernov and the party centre. He advocated a 'businesslike' response to both the formation of the Constituent Assembly and its dissolution. This did not mean underplaying the importance of the Constituent Assembly, but rather recognizing that it was just one arena for democratic struggle. He argued that the SR Party should participate in the elections to the Third Congress of Soviets so as to open up another front, as it were, and also use the right of constituents to recall their soviet deputies to weaken Bolshevik representation; this was done successfully on a number of occasions. Working within the soviets was strengthening the SR party and weakening the Bolsheviks, so the SR Central Committee was relaxed about the dissolution of the Constituent Assembly and called for no armed response in the belief that pressure exerted via the soviets would soon result in its recall.[7]

Red/Green cooperation in the form of the Bolshevik-Left SR coalition administration meant that attention could be turned to the worrying outbreak of 'White' military activity on the Don. Symbolically, the two commanders sent to deal with that problem were the Bolshevik V. Antonov-Ovseenko and the Left SR Muraviev. In the immediate aftermath of the Bolshevik coup many liberal politicians had moved to the Don area, a region where the liberals had always been strong and where the local Cossack leader General A.M. Kaledin had more or less openly sided with Kornilov during his ill-fated coup attempt. First to arrive in the Don area, however, was General M.V. Alekseev, former Commander-in-Chief for the Tsar and the man who had replaced Kornilov after the latter's arrest. He arrived in Novocherkassk on 2 November and at once started forming a Volunteer Army. A month later he was joined by Kornilov himself, who had escaped arrest in the confusion of the October days. The Volunteer Army's first operation took place in Rostov-on-Don. At the end of November an insurrection took place in the city in support of the Soviet Government. The Volunteer Army moved in to suppress it, and after some fierce street fighting succeeded in capturing the town in the first week of December.

The flying corps of the Latvian Riflemen Division, Khodynka Base, 1918. The Latvian force provided crack troops for the Soviet forces.

The Soviet Government was determined to restore the situation, and ordered Antonov-Ovseenko and Muraviev to gather sufficient forces to recapture the city. Their campaign began in earnest in the New Year. Although the White Volunteer Army was disciplined and experienced, it was outnumbered by the Soviet forces which included units from the crack Latvian Riflemen Division. After a steady advance which began on 10 January, Rostov and Novocherkassk were recaptured before the end of February and the Volunteer Army chased into the Kuban. There, on the fringes of Russia, its position steadied. During what became known to its survivors as the Ice March, the Volunteer Army moved across the wild Kuban steppe on the east of the Black Sea in the search for a secure base. First they tried to capture the regional capital Ekaterinodar. Driven back after their initial attack in mid-March, they tried again in early April; this assault was disastrous, since in an artillery exchange a Red shell scored a direct hit on Kornilov's HQ and killed him. Forced to abandon the attempt to capture Ekaterinodar, the White Army, down to three and a half thousand men, marched back into the steppe, eventually finding sanctuary in the middle of May not in the regional capital but in the remote district of Mechetinskaya. While the Soviet Government remained a Bolshevik-Left SR coalition, while the Soviet Government was democratic, the Whites found themselves confined to the very periphery of Russia.[8]

The German Peace and the Path to War

What put Russia back on the path to civil war was the Treaty of Brest Litovsk, signed between the Bolsheviks and the Government of Imperial Germany in March 1918. The Bolshevik-Left SR socialist coalition government, and thus the truce in the Red-Green civil war, broke down on the issue of peace. The process was not immediate. Although the Left SRs left the Bolsheviks to rule alone when the Treaty of Brest Litovsk was ratified on 16 March 1918, they remained in positions of authority within the armed forces and the soviet administration for another three months. They did so because, until early May 1918, there was every expectation that the Bolsheviks would use the treaty with Germany simply as a breathing space and that the struggle against German imperialism would quickly resume. When this did not happen, and it was clear that a socialist coalition administration would never be restored, the Red-Green civil war began in earnest.

The Bolsheviks had not wanted to sign the terms offered them by the Imperial German Government at Brest Litovsk. However, their policy of 'neither peace nor war' was interpreted by the Germans as a rejection of their terms. On 16 February the German Army announced it would resume its offensive on the 18th, and did so when it received no Russian response. By the time the Treaty of Brest Litovsk was signed a fortnight later the Russian Army had been routed and even more harsh conditions imposed on Russia than those originally proposed. During that fourteen day war a patriotic mood swept over the nation. For the 'defence of the socialist fatherland', to use a slogan of the time, the Bolsheviks threw open the prison doors and released many of their political prisoners, including the editorial board of the Right SR paper *Volya naroda*, while the SR Party's military commission volunteered to join the Red Guards in the defence of Petrograd. This mood continued even after Lenin had succeeded in persuading the Bolshevik Central Committee on 23 February that the German terms would have to be accepted. A survey of local soviets carried out from 26 February to 10 March revealed that a majority favoured the war continuing. Lenin was able to stage a Seventh Congress of the Bolshevik Party on 6-7 March, which endorsed the treaty, and a Fourth Congress of Soviets on 14-16 March, which ratified it, but rumours of gerrymandering abounded and even official figures revealed strong anti-treaty feeling on the Volga and in the Urals. Even after ratification, anti-treaty communists continued to be active well into April and May. They controlled the Moscow Regional Party Committee, the Yaroslavl Committee and the Urals Regional Bureau; in Ufa, Perm and Vyatka there were examples of anti-treaty Bolsheviks cooperating with SRs and even Mensheviks in the local soviets. In Ukraine, ceded to Germany under the terms of the treaty, there was never any question but that the communists would try to resist the Germans. Local Red Army forces, led as on the Don by Antonov-Ovseenko and Muraviev, tried to coordinate a policy of partisan warfare to harry the German advance. It was the end of April before the leadership of the Ukrainian communists were forced to seek refuge in Moscow.[9]

Ratification of the Treaty of Brest Litovsk brought the Bolshevik-Left SR socialist coalition to an end. The Left SRs held their Second Congress in Moscow from 17-25 March and voted to establish an Uprising Commission to coordinate partisan activity in Ukraine. Bands of irregular soldiers would regularly slip across the demarcation line between Russian territory and German-occupied Ukraine to carry out guerrilla actions against the Germans. This work was not carried out by the Left SRs alone; the British agent George Hill was actively involved in organizing what he later called 'a splendid band of irregular troops composed of ex-Russian officers' who would cross the border, don peasant garb and help lead the increasing number of Ukrainian peasants prepared to resist German requisitioning units.[10]

The involvement of George Hill in such activities was just one aspect of the Allied policy at this time. While the British had not welcomed the Bolshevik seizure of power, they had responded to it quite calmly, hoping to persuade Lenin to keep at least a token force in the field against Germany; even a weakened Eastern Front could help relive pressure on the Western Front. The German advance of 18 February provided the opportunity to press home this view. Any resistance to Germany would be supported by the Allies, Lenin and his War Minister Trotsky were informed on the 20th. After some hesitation Trotsky persuaded the Central Committee to accept this offer on 22 February, and although the Central Committee agreed to Germany's terms just the next day, on 23 February, it was not immediately clear that Germany intended to respond favourably. As the fate of the treaty hung in the balance, on 29 February and 1 and 2 March, Lenin held talks with Bruce Lockhart, the British agent sent to Russia expressly to counter German influence. Lockhart was optimistic that Russian resistance could be encouraged and that, even if the treaty were eventually signed, the peace would only hold for a matter of weeks.

Lockhart was not the only person to believe that the Treaty of Brest Litovsk could not hold. Lenin had only got his acceptance resolution through the Central Committee on 23 February by threatening to resign and promising that the Bolshevik Party would begin immediate preparations for a revolutionary war; the treaty would provide a breathing space, but the universal assumption was that this would be of short duration. No sooner had the treaty been signed than on 4 March Trotsky began the task of constructing

Red Army bicycle 'commandos' training near Moscow, 1918.

the Red Army; the Supreme War Council he chaired included representatives of the Left SR Party, even though the party had decided to leave the government. The Allies continued to offer aid, and this was enthusiastically accepted; among the experts put at Trotsky's disposal was George Hill, who was given the grand title Inspector of Aviation and the authority to report directly to Trotsky. As part of this wide-ranging brief Hill was also asked to help establish an intelligence network. By the end of March Lockhart was convinced that Trotsky was just waiting for the right moment to restart the war with Germany and by 22 April he had persuaded his masters in London to respond positively.

Having accepted the wisdom of Lockhart's advice, London's problem was how to respond to a Russian request for military aid when there were no troops to spare. The solution came in the form of the Czechoslovak Legion. Given the impossibility of freeing large numbers of troops from the Western Front, the only Allied force of any size which could support Russia's renewed war effort against Germany was the Czechoslovak Legion, since it was already stationed on Russian territory. The Czechoslovak Legion had been recruited from Czech and Slovak prisoners of war captured on the Eastern Front who had previously fought in the Austro-Hungarian Army. The signing of the

Treaty of Brest Litovsk had left them stranded, and they were in the process of moving to the Western Front in France by the only available route – via Siberia, North America and the Atlantic. If the Czechoslovak Legion, now spread out along the railway network from the Volga to Siberia could be moved to the northern port of Archangel, securing *en route* the railway network to the Volga river, it would be ideally placed to welcome any small expeditionary force of British troops sent by sea to Archangel. When the British Government learned that the Czechoslovak Legion had already started to move east it began frantic efforts to convince the leaders of the Czechoslovak Legion that those forces still positioned west of the Ural mountains should not proceed to Vladivostok but to Archangel. With this agreement apparently secured, on 11 May the British cabinet endorsed the proposal that General F.C. Poole set sail for the White Sea, anticipating a welcome from the Czechoslovaks at Archangel and an easy passage down the railway to the strategic city of Vologda. Once there he could galvanize Trotsky's new army to wage renewed war against the Germans.[11]

By the time General Poole actually set sail on 17 May, the situation in Russia had changed completely. The Bolshevik Government had decided against Trotsky's notion that Russia should reopen the Eastern Front with the support of the Allies. It did so because Lenin believed that cooperation with the Allies would erode the Bolsheviks' power base and pressurize them back into a socialist coalition administration. Regional elections in Russia throughout spring 1918 had shown support for the Bolsheviks was ebbing away. Where ever elections were held, the Bolsheviks lost and were only able to retain power by declaring martial law. Even in Petrograd, the cradle of the revolution, the SRs and the Mensheviks succeeded in establishing an Assembly of Factory Delegates which rivaled the soviets as a source of popular authority. Most alarming of all, conferences of Baltic sailors, once the most outspoken pro-Bolshevik group, were passing resolutions in favour of recalling the Constituent Assembly. Chernov's strategy of working through the soviets to undermine support for the Bolsheviks seemed to be working. The various strands of opposition to the Bolsheviks had one thing in common, they were against the Treaty of Brest Litovsk; for Lenin there was a serious danger that, in changing his stance on the treaty the Bolsheviks would be swept aside as new political formations emerged. Both foreign and domestic commentators alike were noting renewed talk of a coalition socialist administration in late April and early May 1918. Lenin preferred the notion of a tacit understanding with the Germans which would enable the Bolsheviks to suspend soviet democracy and rule alone, constructing socialism as they saw fit.[12]

This crisis was precipitated by German action. On 26 April the German ambassador Count Mirbach had arrived in Moscow and immediately made his presence felt by insisting the Treaty of Brest Litovsk be rigorously observed. On 29 April the German authorities in Ukraine overthrew the democratic government which it had tolerated during the first weeks of occupation and imposed a puppet administration headed by Hetman Skoropadskii committed to restoring land to the landlords. To those Bolsheviks opposed to the Treaty of Brest Litovsk, these related actions showed the true face of German imperialism: they insisted the time for resistance had come. The Bolshevik Central Committee then went into a crisis session, which lasted from 6-13 May. In the complex debates Lenin insisted that the 'English ultimatum' be rejected and the Treaty of Brest Litovsk endorsed; Trotsky put the opposing view, but in the end Lenin got his way. Having received reassurances from Berlin that the Bolshevik regime would not share the same fate as that of the Ukrainian democrats, the Central Committee decided to continue relying on German support, and agreed to Lenin's proposal that it was necessary to underpin that support by immediately holding talks about future bilateral trade.[13]

Having secured German protection through a reinforced separate peace, Lenin could, he believed, resume the struggle against the enemies of proletarian power and set about constructing socialism. He could get back to where he had wanted to be in October 1917. Freed from reliance on his Left SR coalition partners, Lenin could impose socialism according to his understanding of Marxism. That meant above all industrial growth through such policies as the introduction of economic planning, one-man management of factories, and the employment of former 'bourgeois' specialists. Constructing socialism also meant radical changes in agrarian policy. The Bolshevik-Left SR coalition government had given the peasants the land. The Left SRs believed that, thereafter, state grain needs could be secured by trading with the peasants at reasonable prices – 'firm' prices, to use the language of the day.

The Bolsheviks, whose Marxism taught them that there were both rich and poor peasants, felt that the rich peasants, or 'kulaks' would exploit such a free trade in grain. For the Bolsheviks, socialism meant an end to free trade, an end to what they termed speculation; in their vision of the socialist future, the peasants would voluntarily surrender their grain to the industrial working class in return for industrial goods. When peasants began to protest at such policies, Lenin decided to give his rural poor an organizational voice. For Lenin, those peasants who demanded the right to sell their grain were rich peasants, kulaks, who could be countered by launching a class war against them, a class war led by the poor peasants and their committees. The class war started on 9 May when a decree was passed under which units of workers were empowered to go out to the countryside and collect grain by force, hopefully bringing poor peasants over to their side and striking jointly against rich 'kulaks'. A supplementary decree of 11 June set up the Poor Peasants' Committees, which had the dual role of being agents of Bolshevik power in the village and splitting the peasants into the categories desired by the government. Lenin needed to establish the Poor Peasants' Committees because the vast majority of village soviets remained firmly in the hands of the Left SRs who opposed this policy of grain requisitioning.

Green versus Red Civil War

By the end of May it was clear to the SRs that the Bolshevik government was anti-democratic, because it had dissolved the Constituent Assembly; anti-peasant, because of the formation of the Poor Peasants' Committees; and pro-German, because of its decision to bolster the Treaty of Brest Litovsk with economic talks. Yet the civil war between the Bolsheviks and the SRs started in a way nobody had planned. In line with their new pro-German stance, the Bolsheviks agreed to a German request that the Czechoslovak Legion should be disarmed, and moves to this end began on 15 May. Unaware of the change in the Bolsheviks' stance, and fulfilling the request of the Allies, also on 15 May the leaders of the Czechoslovak Legion ordered that the bulk of the Legion's First Division, scattered along the railway network from Penza to Chelyabinsk, should redeploy towards Archangel. The Czechoslovak commanders on the ground, aware of Trostky's disarmament call and assuming its own leadership was out of touch with the most recent developments, refused to proceed to Archangel, since this would mean performing a U-turn and heading back towards those Bolshevik forces which wished to disarm them. Thus, at a conference held on 21-23 May in Chelyabinsk, the Czechoslovak Legion voted to ignore an impassioned plea from an Allied emissary, who no doubt pointed out that General Poole was about to drop anchor in the White Sea, and resolved to continue their journey east.

As the Czechoslovak Legion moved east, so its soldiers met local soviets now under instructions from Trotsky to disarm them. Clashes were inevitable, clashes which could only benefit the SR Party, for many of the Czechoslovak trains were travelling through the Volga region, the traditional heartland of the SR Party. At the very start of June the Constituent Assembly deputies for Samara met together secretly and agreed to make an approach to the local Czechoslovak military commander: if, they suggested, the local SR militia and the Czechoslovak soldiers acted together, Samara could be captured and the Czechoslovaks would be free to travel east while the SRs would have gained control of an important regional centre. The Czechoslovaks took some persuading, but once the SR militia had already begun its assault and succeeded in securing a crucial bridge, the Czechoslovaks decided to commit themselves. On 8 June Samara fell, and the local SR Constituent Assembly deputies decided to make the town the base for a new anti-Bolshevik government which they called the Committee of the Constituent Assembly, or 'Komuch'. A week later the former Navy Minister Lebedev arrived in Samara and was given the task of turning the small SR militia into a People's Army.[14]

Lebedev had been sent to the area by an organization called the Union for the Regeneration of Russia (URR). The URR was made up of those right-wing SRs who had always supported Kerensky in his twin policies of supporting the war effort and collaborating with liberal politicians. Among its leading figures were Kerensky's former Deputy Minister of War Boris Savinkov, the editor of *Volya naroda* Pitirim Sorokin and Lebedev himself. Equally well represented were Popular Socialists like Chaikovskii. They responded to the Bolshevik decision of 13 May by convening an underground conference of Constituent Assembly deputies and urging the Allies to try to open a new Eastern Front on the river Volga. Understandably it was to this group that the Allies turned once it was clear that Trotsky's proposal for cooperation had been rejected. Breaking his contacts with Trotsky, Lockhart turned instead to the URR. With no Czechoslovak troops *en route* to Archangel because of the mutiny of the Czechoslovak Legion, General Poole's descent from Archangel to the Volga would be extremely difficult. It could be eased by a series of insurrections, crucially in Archangel itself and also in Yaroslavl and the upper Volga.

In talks between Lockhart and the URR these insurrections were initially scheduled for the first week in July. The Archangel insurrection was to be the work of Sorokin and Chaikovskii; they were to enter the city together and Chaikovskii was to head the new interim administration envisaged by the URR, bearing the name of the Directory. As Sorokin and Chaikovskii neared Archangel the news came through that Poole had had to delay his landing since promised reinforcements from Britain had not yet materialized. Unfortunately this message did not get through to Boris Savinkov, the organizer of the insurrection in Yaroslavl. Unaware that the Archangel landing had been postponed his forces began operations on 4 July. Without the support of the Allies it was a doomed enterprise; fighting continued until 20 July, but ultimately the insurgents were forced to surrender. Meanwhile on the Volga the new People's Army was desperately trying to make headway northwards to rendezvous with any anti-Bolshevik forces able to make the journey south from Archangel. After the bitterest of fighting Lebedev took, lost and finally retook Syzran on 10 July. By then the leaders of the Czechoslovak Legion had finally been convinced that it was official Allied policy to support the SR insurrection. As a consequence significant Czechoslovak forces were deployed to support the People's Army which mounted a full-scale assault on Kazan, finally taking the city on 8 August.[15]

Not only did Lenin face a 'Green' civil war launched by the main stream of the SR Party, but he faced an insurrection from his former allies, the Left SRs. When the fighting had begun the Bolsheviks had excluded the SRs and the Mensheviks from the soviets. This decree of 14 June did not, however, effect the Left SRs, who still hoped to remove Lenin from power democratically. On the basis of their peasant support, the Left SRs had anticipated winning the elections to the Fifth Congress of Soviets, delegates to which gathered in Moscow in the first week of July 1918. Their plan had been to use their electoral victory not only to change Lenin's peasant policy but to launch a

Members of the Red Latvian Riflemen Division taking up position before the Bolshoi Theatre, Moscow, at the time of the Left SR insurrection, 6 July 1918.

revolutionary war against imperial Germany. The Bolshevik decision to allow representation at the Congress of Soviets from delegates elected by the Poor Peasants' Committees deprived the Left SRs of that victory. Frustrated at the Bolsheviks' gerrymandering, the Left SRs decided to resort to direct action. On 6 July they assassinated the German ambassador Count Mirbach and staged an insurrection in the capital. Although ultimately unsuccessful, the insurgents did control Moscow's telegraph building long enough to appeal for support from the rest of the country.[16] This appeal was received sympathetically in many of the soviets of the Volga region and prompted the commander of the Red Army confronting Lebedev's People's Army to rebel and establish an insurrectionary HQ in Simbirsk; from there he called for cooperation with the Czechoslovak Legion in declaring war on Germany.

The commander of the Red Army on the Volga front was Muraviev, the same man who had led the forces opposed to Kerensky at Pulkovo Heights and had helped rout the White Generals on the Don. A Left SR for much of the time since October, he had flirted with anarchism during his time in Ukraine when he and Antonov-Ovseenko had tried to delay the German occupation. Muraviev was known to be deeply troubled by the Treaty of Brest Litovsk and had once before called for cooperation with the Czechoslovak Legion; from mid-February to mid-March his military actions against the

Defensive measures at the Kremlin, Moscow, summer 1918.

Germans in Ukraine had been conducted in cooperation with the Czechoslovaks. Although Muraviev was killed on 10 July at the very start of his rebellion, its impact was devastating. The only disciplined force among the Red Army units on the Volga front was the Fourth Regiment of Latvian Riflemen. The Fourth Regiment was uncertain whether or not to support Muraviev. After contacting Moscow they learned that it had been the commander of the Latvian Riflemen Division, I.I. Vacietis, who had put down the Left SR insurrection in Moscow, and as a reward he had been made the new commander on the Volga Front. On the other hand, they knew that some of the forces most loyal to Muraviev were other Latvian units which had followed him from the Don to Ukraine, fighting the Germans all the way. Like in all the other Latvian regiments the great bulk of the riflemen were peasants, deeply suspicious of the new policy of grain requisitioning introduced by Lenin and alarmed at the activities of the Poor Peasants' Committees. In the end the Fourth Regiment had had enough of fighting for Lenin's vision of socialism. It withdrew from Syzran in good order, but then simply refused to act; orders to move to defend Simbirsk were ignored and by 23 July more than a quarter of the regiment had been disarmed for refusing to carry out orders. With little difficulty the People's Army took Simbirsk on 22 July from where their successful assault on Kazan was launched.

Red Latvian Riflemen outside Kazan on 5 August 1918, the eve of the city's capture by the People's Army.

The fall of Kazan caused near panic in Bolshevik ranks. Not only did the People's Army capture the city, but in so doing gained control of the country's gold reserves which had been evacuated there for safe-keeping. Trotsky was *en route* to sort out the crisis as Kazan fell. When he arrived at the Red Army base of Sviyazhsk just outside Kazan on 12 August for his first discussions with Vacietis, the issue of the Fourth Regiment still had not been resolved. When its commander threatened 'consequences dangerous to the revolution' if the regiment was not recalled from the front, Trotsky had him arrested. It was outside Kazan that the Red Army began the practice of executing one in ten men from those units which refused to obey orders. Such drastic measures had their impact but it was 1 September before the First and Sixth Latvian Regiments arrived at the front and the situation outside Kazan was stable enough to think about a counter-offensive.[17]

Meanwhile the Allies were doing everything they could to support the Green side and establish a government committed to fighting the war with Germany to a successful conclusion. General Poole landed in Archangel on 2 August and advanced towards his twin goals, Vologda along the railway line and Kotlas along the river Dvina; the first would give access to the river Volga and the second to the Trans-Siberian railway. By the middle of August the general was optimistic about achieving both goals. To smooth his path Lockhart had developed a new strategy. Reports of the questionable loyalty of the Latvian Riflemen had begun to circulate in the diplomatic community. With the support of George Hill efforts were made in August to strengthen Allied influence amongst those Latvians stationed both on the Volga and at Vologda. Morale among the Latvians in Vologda was particularly low as Poole's forces approached, and Lockhart sought to put Poole in touch with dissident Latvian commanders who might come over to his side. The assassination attempt on Lenin's life on 30 August, followed by Lockhart's arrest, put an effective end to this attempt to subvert the Latvians further.[18]

Building a Green Government

The first round in the Red-Green civil war had clearly gone to the Greens; militarily the People's Army and its British and Czechoslovak allies looked in a strong position towards the end of August. However, political divisions within the Green camp helped stall that military advance and give the second round in the Red-Green civil war to the Bolsheviks. In autumn 1918 all the political disagreements which had dogged the SRs during 1917 resurfaced. The most important of these was the attitude to be adopted towards the liberals. The Right SR dominated URR, whose emissary to London was Kerensky himself, had never made any secret of its commitment to the Allies and its willingness to cooperate with left-leaning liberals. They wanted a return to Kerensky's Third Coalition Government. The SR Central Committee, on the other hand, felt that the lesson of 1917 had been clear; there was no advantage in an alliance with liberals. More than that, even if there had once been a need to ally with the liberals, that was no longer the case since the Constituent Assembly elections had shown conclusively that the SR Party had a popular mandate to rule alone.

The SR Central Committee was equally cautious about too close an association with the Allies. At the Eighth Party Conference held in Moscow in May 1918 it had been agreed that there was a difference between cooperating with the Allies in the struggle against Germany and cooperating with the Allies in a domestic civil war with the Bolsheviks. The first was permissible, the second impermissible. As more and more SR Constituent Assembly delegates gathered in Samara and the Party's Central Committee moved its base there, the Allies found their reception was becoming cooler. Although one Menshevik did join the Komuch administration – I.V. Maiskii, later the Soviet ambassador to Britain on the eve of the Second World War, was Departmental Director of Labour – all the others were SRs, including Departmental Director for Trade and Industry V.N. Filippovskii. His appointment to a post liberals might have coveted reflected the fact that Komuch was unashamedly socialist in its outlook. Although some factories 'prematurely' nationalized by the Bolsheviks were denationalized, Komuch retained most Bolshevik labour legislation, established committees and commissions to oversee the economy, and retained such external trappings of revolution as red flags. In addition the People's Army wore only plain coloured epaulettes and the salary of officers was linked to that of a worker's wage.[19]

Such revolutionary purism was not shared by the new political leaders of other parts of Russia where soviet power had been overthrown by the Czechoslovak Legion. Since Czechoslovak units were spread out along the whole of the Trans-Siberian Railway, most major cities fell into this category. Not all these towns recognized the authority of Komuch and this was partly the fault of Komuch itself. It had always been SR policy to establish a federal Russia, and a degree of regional autonomy for Siberia had always been in their programme. When the Constituent Assembly had been dissolved in January 1918 the SRs in Siberia had summoned a Siberian Regional Assembly which, before being dispersed by the Bolsheviks, established a Siberian regional government composed of SRs. This government had retained a shadowy authority despite Bolshevik rule, for the cooperative movement was extremely strong in western Siberia and had provided a cover for some of its activities. Thus, when the Czechoslovak Legion rebelled, the Siberian Government simply emerged from hiding and took up the reigns of power.

To the consternation of many SRs, the Siberian Government, once re-established, dissociated itself from the Siberian Regional Assembly which had appointed it; at the same time it made clear it no longer felt bound to implement the SR programme. Only one member of the government, B.M. Shatilov, considered himself responsible in any way to the Party's Central Committee. The others had fallen under the sway of I.A. Mikhailov whose experience as director of the Economic Council of the Provisional Government and secretary to the liberal minister A.I. Shingarev had turned him against all socialist experimentation. Mikhailov was an SR by repute only. He lived in the political shadow of his father who had been exiled for his terrorist activities. Later he became active in the SR Party during the elections to the Second Imperial State Duma in 1907. Another government member, P.V. Vologodskii, had also been elected to the Second Duma, before dropping out of political life. These men were chosen to join the Siberian Government in January 1918 – as Bolshevik forces closed in and reputations were all the anxious delegates to the Siberian Regional Assembly had to go on – but the choices they made were extremely unfortunate for the SR cause. The restored Siberian Government of June 1918 had nothing in common with SR policy; it dissolved all soviets and land committees, restored private ownership and private trade, and refused to recognize that Komuch, supposedly the voice of the Constituent Assembly, had any authority in Omsk, its chosen seat of government. On 4 July it declared that Siberia, with its western border tantalizingly undefined, was independent until a future All-Russian administration could be formed. The political sympathies of the Siberian Government were far closer to the liberals than the SRs.[20]

It was the URR and the Allies, both committed to recreating the Third Coalition Government that tried to smooth over this burgeoning dog-fight between the SR government in Samara and the liberal government in Omsk. A URR emissary arrived in Samara on 11 July and tried to persuade a sceptical audience that the important thing was not to assert the authority of the government in Samara or the government in Omsk, but to move to the creation of an All-Russian Government which all could recognize. Reluctantly a Komuch delegation travelled to Chelyabinsk where an equally truculent delegation from the Siberian Government had assembled. To the bewilderment of Allied representatives, the two delegations sat in their trains in adjacent sidings and communicated only through written notes. It was only when the French officer present, a Major Guinet, suggested that a joint photograph be taken that direct talks began on 15 July.

Although both sides eventually agreed to the summoning of a State Conference in Chelyabinsk in early August to resolve their differences, on their return to their respective capitals both delegations tried to manoeuvre for position. First to act was the Siberian Government which established a customs border between its territory and that of Komuch, annexing towns claimed by Komuch as it did so. In response Komuch claimed that, since it owed its sovereignty to the Constituent Assembly it was the only national government, while the Siberian Government's jurisdiction was purely regional. Komuch politicians hinted darkly that they might not, after all, attend the state conference in Chelyabinsk. If the groups invited to the Chelyabinsk conference had been limited simply to the Samara and Omsk administrations this might well have been the result, but the Allies and the URR had persuaded both sides that the Siberian Regional Assembly should also be invited to send delegates. This gave the Samara SRs hope that the power of the Omsk Government could be sapped from within; the Siberian Regional Assembly would be the Omsk government's Achilles heel. The SRs had a clear majority in the reformed Siberian Regional Assembly, an organization to which the Siberian Government was still, nominally at least, responsible.

If the invitation to the Siberian Regional Assembly was a carrot for Komuch to attend the Chelyabinsk conference, the Allies also offered an inducement to the Siberian Government. The Allies decided to establish a third regional government in the area, at Ekaterinburg. This Urals Government was established on 1 August. Komuch responded as expected by denouncing it and encouraging the local population to oppose it. The Siberian Government, as the Allies had hoped, was conciliatory. It agreed to the Urals Government attending the Chelyabinsk Conference in return for an agreement to coordinate military strategy and all movement along the Trans-Siberian Railway. Thus when the Chelyabinsk State Conference opened on 23 August, two weeks after the planned opening date, the hard work of the Allies and the

URR began to pay off. Despite some back-biting amongst the delegates, it was agreed that all interested parties should attend a further meeting in Ufa which would establish once and for all an All-Russian Government. The man elected chairman was Avksentiev, the former chairman of the Preparliament, who had made his way to Chelyabinsk from the north through Perm, trudging on foot for a whole fortnight through wild, marshy country.[21]

The Ufa State Conference was a further triumph for the URR. It opened on 8 September, again under the chairmanship of Avksentiev, and after nearly two weeks of discussion all sides recognized the formation on 23 September of a five-member Directory; this body would hold power until a new Constituent Assembly could be summoned. The composition of the Directory was entirely to the liking of the URR, and far less to the liking of both the liberals and the SRs. It was, in essence, the successful recreation of Kerensky's Third Coalition Government. The five members were: Avksentiev; General V.G. Boldyrev, a Right SR; Zenzinov, a member of the SR Central Committee; and V.A. Vinogradov, a Siberian liberal. For many SRs, this return to Kerenskyism was a step too far, but V.K. Volskii, the leader of the Komuch delegation to the Ufa State Conference, was determined to work for a compromise. So it was agreed that the Directory now formed would appoint an All-Russian Government to administer the country. There then remained the question of the existing governments in Ekaterinburg, Omsk and Samara. The solution adopted here was easy to grasp in outline: Komuch was to become a regional government for the Volga region, the Urals Government would become a regional government for the Urals region; and the Siberian Government would become a regional government for Siberia. However, the detail of these interweaving sovereignties was still being addressed as the Ufa State Conference came to a close and it was left to the goodwill of all concerned to resolve them.[22]

White Machinations

If the return to Kerenskyism caused unease among members of the SR Central Committee, it caused consternation among reactionary White army officers. It was not long before Kornilov-style coup plotting resumed, and the first such incident occurred in Archangel. The URR had planned to establish a Directory long before the Ufa State Conference could be assembled and its initial candidate to chair that body had been Chaikovskii; hence it was Chaikovskii who was dispatched to Archangel to accompany General Poole in what was expected to be a victorious march south. When that advance did not materialize Chaikovskii established a civilian administration in Archangel which gave all but one of the ministerial posts to SRs; these included such long term associates as Dedusenko, S.S. Maslov and M.A. Likhach. The tenor of Chaikovskii's administration was opitimized by the daily paper it produced; called *The Regeneration of the North* the very title echoed the commitment of all ministers to the URR, while the paper retained the masthead slogan 'Workers of All Countries Unite!' This radicalism was incomprehensible to General Poole and Chaikovskii soon found himself at loggerheads with Poole over the question of whether it was appropriate for the new administration to continue flying the red flag. Later, given Chaikovskii's long concern for questions of social justice, he was soon involved in a long dispute with Poole as to whether or not martial law should be declared and whether or not military courts had the right to impose the death penalty.

Against this background of tension between the Allies' military representative and Chaikovskii's civilian administration it is scarcely surprising that White officers began to scheme. In particular they resented the activities of Maslov, the man given the defence portfolio. The stand-off lasted several weeks. Frustrated by a policy of non-cooperation from the newly established Archangel military staff, and determined he was to have some say over military appointments, Maslov decided to sack the Archangel commandant and replaced him with a military governor; the man proposed was Maslov's close friend, and Constituent Assembly deputy, Dedusenko. This was to wave a red rag to a bull. On 5 September the Commander of the Archangel Armed Forces staged a coup. Chaikovskii and his fellow ministers were arrested and taken to the Solovetskii Island Monastery in the White Sea, later to become one of the most infamous Soviet prison camps. At this point Allied representatives intervened, and forced the commander to return the ministers to Archangel. They tried to broker a compromise, which would have involved some, but not all, of Chaikovskii's ministers moving to other posts. Rather than accept this compromise, Chaikovskii resigned on 12 September. News had reached him of the opening of the Ufa State Conference and the appointment of the Directory, and Chaikovskii was determined that the administration of Northern Russia should be in the hands of this newly established All-Russian Government. To finalize such an arrangement Maslov, Likhach and Dedusenko left Archangel for the hazardous journey to Siberia.[23]

To White officers, moderate socialists like Chaikovskii, and even more so the actual Directory leader Avksentiev, were simply representatives of Kerensky's Provisional Government. Just as in the north, so too in Siberia machinations by White officers became a feature of political life. At the same time as the Ufa State Conference took place, the long promised Siberian Regional Assembly opened in Tomsk on 10 September. Members of its SR majority immediately launched a campaign to restore democratic control over the Siberian Government, acting with the support of two Siberian government ministers, B.M. Shatilov and G.B. Patushinskii. The latter had just resigned his post in protest at the increasingly dictatorial behaviour of Mikhailov and the 'administrative council' he used as his power base. The Siberian Government responded to this challenge by announcing the dissolution of the Siberian Regional Assembly. To prevent this decision being implemented a delegation from the Siberian Regional Assembly came to Omsk on 18 September to confront Mikhailov in person. Mikhailov found himself outnumbered by Shatilov, another Siberian Government minister who had tired of Mikhailov, V.M. Krutovskii, and A.E. Novoselov. In January 1918 Novoselov had been appointed Minister of the Interior in the Siberian Government but because he had fled to Vladivostok during the period of Bolshevik rule, he had thus far not been able to help in re-establishing the Siberian Government; once secure travel was possible along the entire length of the Trans-Siberian Railway, Novoselov, a committed SR, travelled to Omsk not merely to take up his place in the Siberian Government but to boost its SR colours. Mikhailov's response to this challenge was to carry out a coup of sorts. Novoselov was found dead on 21 September after being detained by Mikhailov's Security Department. The next day, on 22 September, Krutovskii and Shatilov, with guns held to their heads, agreed to resign from the Siberian Government, leaving all power in the hands of Mikhailov.[24]

This brutal murder of one minister and the enforced resignation of two others was the first issue to be addressed by the newly established Directory. On 24 September it ordered the reinstatement of the ministers who had 'resigned', but, to balance things, agreed that the suspension of the Siberian Regional Assembly had been lawful. A Directory representative was sent to Omsk to investigate whether any criminal offences had taken place, but a report from the Czechoslovak Legion showing Mikhailov's direct involvement in the murder was shelved. The Directory subsequently regretted not having dealt with Mikhailov when it had the chance.

One of the things left vague after the Ufa State Conference had concluded its work was whether the Directory and its All-Russian Government, or the various regional governments, would be responsible for communications, including the rail and telegraph systems. It seemed a trivial matter, but when the Directory moved to Omsk to take up residence, it immediately became clear that they had been mistaken to believe that such details could be left to be resolved through good will. In Omsk the Directory discovered that Mikhailov's Siberian Government claimed to control the communications network. Mikhailov's clear ambition was to secure influence over whom the Directory appointed All-Russian ministers by insisting that the offices of the Siberian Government, in particular his Administrative Council, were included in any such discussions. To gain the administrative apparatus it needed, the Directory risked losing the right to appoint ministers. Ultimately Mikhailov's strategy worked, the Directory had no choice but to come to an understanding with the Administrative Council.[25]

Green Victory?

It took two weeks for the tussle over the appointment of ministers to be resolved. In the event most ministerial appointments proved uncontroversial.

Admiral Kolchak, who arrived in Omsk on 13 October after reaching Vladivostok a month earlier from the United States, was appointed Minister of War with no objection from the People's Army Commander in Chief and Directory member General Boldyrev. The only controversial appointment was that of Minister of the Interior. The Directory wanted to appoint E.F. Rogovskii, who had been Departmental Director for State Security in the Komuch administration. The Administrative Council protested: it was universally felt in Omsk that Rogovskii, with his personal security force, might strengthen the hand of the SRs too much. In response to this suggestion, the Administrative Council demanded that Mikhailov should be made Minister of Finance. After threats of resignation a compromise of sorts was reached. Mikhailov would be Minister of Finance and Rogovskii Deputy Minister of the Interior with responsibility for security issues and the right to attend cabinet meetings.

This was the Directory's last concession. A month had passed since the Directory had been established, but once its ministerial team was appointed the stranglehold of the Administrative Council could be broken. On 2 November the Urals Government surrendered its authority to the Directory, and on 4 November the Siberian Government did the same. As junior government posts began to be filled the number of SRs appointed steadily rose, balancing the number of former Siberian Government ministers who held first rank posts. More importantly, when the All-Russian Government met for the first time on 5 November it learnt that the Directory proposed to have no cabinet system; the task of the new ministers was simply to administer and serve the Directory, which would retain the right to legislate in its own right. In foreign affairs in particular, Avksentiev insisted that all matters related exclusively to the Directory and were his concern alone. The Directory was determined to break out of the straight jacket Mikhailov had tried to impose.[26]

Confronting the former Siberian Government was only one side of the Directory's work. Just as Kerensky's Third Coalition Government had faced problems from both liberals and SRs, so Mikhailov's campaign against the Directory was mirrored by antagonism from the SR Party. At first the party had gone along with the decision to dissolve Komuch and turn it into a purely regional administration. It began the task on 13 October by establishing a four-member commission, which included Filippovskii, to administer the residual 'national' tasks, essentially organizing the railway and armed forces, until the new All-Russian national ministries were established by the Directory. This much was done without protest, but the mood changed when the surviving deputies to the Constituent Assembly met in congress on 14 October. Many deputies were extremely unhappy with the way the Directory had been established: news from Omsk of the disagreement between the Directory and the Administrative Council made them even angrier. When the SR Party Central Committee met, it decided to condemn the decision of those attending the Ufa State Conference to establish the Directory. Then on 22 October the

Central Committee called on party members to make military preparations to frustrate what it saw as the imminent danger of a right-wing coup. In this new climate Komuch suddenly announced that it would not, after all, abandon its claim to be a national government and would not turn itself into a purely regional administration. In particular, it insisted on retaining the right to form a military force of its own, establishing volunteer units known as Constituent Assembly battalions. Not surprisingly, General Boldyrev protested immediately since it was clearly understood that only the Directory now had the power to command an army, even though, as Komuch liked to point out, the new volunteer military units had done much to stabilize the front.

In the ensuing row the Directory stood firm. Zenzinov, the one member of the Directory who was still a member of the SR Central Committee, worked day and night to defuse the situation. He won the support of many sections of the party in condemning those Constituent Assembly deputies who had protested at the formation of the Directory; he patiently explained to Chernov that the danger of a right-wing coup had passed and that calling for military moves to prevent it only made the situation worse; and by 15 November he had browbeaten Komuch into reaching an acceptable compromise on its future as a regional administration. Indeed, by 15 November the troubles of the Directory seemed to be over. It had succeeded in turning the tables on the Siberian Government as well as persuading a truculent SR Party that compromise was the best way forward. On 16 November even better news was received: the British cabinet had decided to recognize the Directory as the legitimate government of Russia. These political triumphs were mirrored by success on the battlefield, for, after a period of retreat, at the start of November 1918 the People's Army began a successful counter-offensive.[27]

The military situation had changed dramatically since the People's Army had captured Kazan. On 27 August 1918 Lenin signed a trade treaty with Imperial Germany. In return for grain exports and industrial concessions, Lenin had bought the secure knowledge that there would be no fighting in the west. All available troops could therefore be transferred to the east to prepare for the reconquest of Kazan. This was the time when the Bolshevik Government was at its most ruthless. Unlike the Directory, torn hither and thither by internal dissension, the Bolshevik Party showed the iron discipline for which it was to become famous. The unsuccessful assassination attempt on Lenin's life of 30 August was followed by the Red Terror, which by the end of October had claimed at least 10,000 victims, executed as sympathizers with the *ancien régime*.[28]

At the same time, after a massive build up, the Red Army launched its offensive against Kazan and on 8 September recaptured the city. From there they moved to Samara, approaching the city on 19 September. However, this was a more difficult nut to crack and it was only on 6 October that the city was finally captured. Then, as the Bolsheviks advanced towards Ufa, their progress was slowed even more noticeably. Whatever the political wisdom of Komuch forming its own volunteer units they proved their worth in blunting the Red

Red Army machine-gunners in Western Siberia, autumn 1918.

Army's attack. Indeed, by the end of October the Red Army's advance had clearly run out of steam. Colonel Leo Steveni, a British intelligence officer who toured the front at this time, noted that those fighting the Bolsheviks were meeting 'considerable success'. Units formed by the Siberian Government were beginning to advance along the Trans-Siberian Railway towards Perm; worker volunteers from the town of Izhevsk were advancing under General S.N. Voitsekhovskii to the south of the railway; and still further south General V.O. Kappel was operating with the Kazan and Samara Divisions of the People's Army turning the front back towards Samara.[29]

On 10 November the commander of the Red Army's eastern front received the following panicky telegram:

> The enemy has launched an offensive with overwhelming force at Kandry Station [approximately 220 miles east of Samara]. We bring to the attention of the Front that since we were given orders to capture Ufa we have been deprived of the following units [details omitted]: thus, currently able to undertake serious operations, there are six regiments and five batteries, most of which were formed as the planned operations against Ufa developed. We bring to your notice that this puts us in an

Colonel Leo Steveni, who toured the front in the autumn of 1918, pictured while guiding British Embassy staff to safety in Finland in February of the same year.

impossible situation… Send an immediate answer and allow us to regroup our forces.[30]

The Directory's counter-offensive was well underway and Avksentiev could afford to be a little complacent. During a visit to Tomsk on 15 November, for talks with former members of the Siberian Regional Assembly, Avksentiev oozed confidence, composure and optimism. An old student friend, who by 1918 had become an active Zionist, recalled meeting him that day.

Whom should I come upon by chance in one of the main streets of Tomsk, but Avksentiev himself, being driven in a handsome open cab, drawn by a fine pair of horses. He was wearing an overcoat with a fur collar, worn well opened, and hat less, to reveal his long light auburn hair, worn with a centre parting.. and small beard... How vivid to me to this day is the sight of him as he drove along, the Directory displaying its newly elected head. I was of course duly impressed, feeling that here at last, after a troublesome gestation, I was meeting the Russia of the future. In our hearts at the time, the establishment of the Directory symbolized the end of the horrors of civil war.[31]

But the civil war was not to end so easily in Lenin's defeat. During the night of 17-18 November, Admiral Kolchak staged a coup, deposing the Directory and arresting its members. Ironically, included among those caught in Kolchak's net were the three delegates from Chaikovskii's Archangel administration, who had just reached Omsk after a journey lasting almost two months. When the three had been arrested by the military in Archangel, the British had intervened to free them. There were no Allied forces of similar size in Omsk. The small British contingent could do no more than mitigate its worst consequences. It was made clear to Kolchak and his backers that if any harm came to the arrested Directory members there would be no Allied support whatsoever for the new White administration.[32]

TWO

Red Victory?

Admiral Kolchak's coup changed the nature of Russia's civil war. Although the Whites had played a part in the fighting of 1917-18, it had been only a minor part. While the Bolsheviks and Left SR coalition – a Red-Green coalition – had remained intact the Whites had been confined to the Kuban and other distant regions of the country. What broke the Bolshevik-Left SR alliance was the Treaty of Brest Litovsk. This united all SR opinion against the Bolsheviks, giving the Greens a crystal clear democratic mandate which the Allies could enthusiastically endorse. The result was the Directory, the re-embodiment of Kerensky's democratic republic, fighting against German militarism.

Kolchak's coup deprived the anti-Bolshevik forces of their democratic mandate and drove the Greens back towards the Reds; after Kolchak's coup the vast majority of SRs found it impossible to contemplate any further contact with liberals. In its second stage the Russia's civil war would be like the skirmishes on the Don in 1918, a fight between the Whites and an uneasy alliance of Reds and Greens. What made such an alliance possible, for all its instability, was not only the presence of a common enemy, Kolchak, but also the fact that the First World War had ended. By mid-November 1918 the Treaty of Brest Litovsk, which had done so much to separate Reds from Greens, was a thing of the past.

The end of the First World War, however, had a contradictory impact on Bolshevik-SR relations. The defeat of Germany, Austria-Hungary and Turkey set off revolutions throughout Europe. While, to borrow the Bolsheviks' Marxist language, most of these revolutions got no further than the democratic stage of establishing parliamentary regimes, there were moments, particularly in spring 1919, when a European socialist revolution looked a possibility. On those occasions the Bolsheviks, looking to their future relations with a German socialist utopia, prepared to put Marxist orthodoxy in agrarian policy above the day-to-day necessities of their own peasantry.

Revenge on the SRs

Preparations for Kolchak's coup had been carefully laid. As Novoselov's murder in September 1918 had made clear, the key to success was the attitude of the

Czechoslovak Legion. On that occasion, when White army officers had detained SR members of the Siberian Government, the Czechoslovak Legion had acted quickly to restore order and had even wanted to arrest Mikhailov as the instigator of the plot and put him on trial. For Kolchak's coup to succeed the Czechoslovak Legion would have to be neutralized. So, one of Kolchak's most prominent liberal supporters toured Siberia denouncing the agreement made at the Ufa State Conference and lobbying support for the alternative of a military dictatorship. On 28 September he had talks in Vladivostok with Rudolf Gajda, the Czechoslovak general who had led the June revolt against the Bolsheviks and had gained control of the entire Trans-Siberian Railway. The two men not only agreed that there should be a dictatorship, but that Kolchak was the best candidate. Gajda undertook to ensure that the Czechoslovak Legion would not oppose the coup and he was as true as his word. On the eve of the coup Gajda, now based in Ekaterinburg, repeated his promise of Czechoslovak neutrality. As Kolchak took over the reigns of power, the Czechoslovak Legion took no action and the only force which might have come to the aid of the Directory, the Battalion of State Defence led by the SR Deputy Minister of the Interior, Rogovskii, was surrounded and disarmed.[1]

SRs throughout Siberia felt betrayed. In an appeal to the Czechoslovak National Council, sent from Ufa on 23 November 1918 and copied to President Masaryk of Czechoslovakia, the survivors of the Komuch administration, officially still the regional government for the Volga, asked that the Czechoslovaks respond to this coup against a government which they had helped establish; Komuch urged them to repudiate the coup and to support those armed units which remained loyal to the Constituent Assembly. In Ekaterinburg the surviving members of the Constituent Assembly held a joint meeting with members of the SR Party Central Committee. Both issued a protest and formed an Extraordinary Committee of Opposition, which included party leader Chernov and Volskii, who had led the SR delegation to the Ufa State Conference. Without Czechoslovak support, however, their threat to send an 'Allied-Russian' force to overthrow Kolchak remained an empty one: opposition was impossible. Only those Czechoslovaks most closely associated with the SR Party acted to mitigate the extent of the disaster.[2]

In Ekaterinburg the local members of the Czechoslovak National Council came out in support of Chernov. Later, Czechoslovak units saved his life when, on 19 November, White officers stormed the Palais Royale Hotel where Chernov was based; in the fighting one member of the Constituent Assembly was killed, but those taken prisoner, who included Chernov, Volskii and others, were saved from summary execution by the arrival of a Czechoslovak unit. The Czechoslovak National Council then intervened to ensure that these prisoners were taken not to Omsk, home of Kolchak's government, but to Ufa, where the former Komuch administration still had some authority. That quasi-autonomy did not last long. On 30 November Kolchak issued 'Order 56' which called on his army commanders to use force to end the activities of the former Komuch administration and those associated with it. Chernov and Volskii managed to escape, but on 2 December some twenty-seven other leading SRs were arrested in Ufa and transferred to Omsk. Amongst those arrested was Filippovskii, former Komuch Minister for Trade and Industry.[3]

In the early months of Kolchak's rule, revenge against the SRs dominated all aspects of state policy. For foreign consumption a trial was held on 21 November of the three officers accused of organizing the coup; they admitted their role but the court accepted their defence, that they had acted to preempt an SR insurrection. They were therefore acquitted and the vendetta against the SRs continued. What ultimate fate Kolchak had for them is uncertain, but they fell victims to the bloodlust of White officers. On 21 December the Bolsheviks in Omsk tried to stage a workers' insurrection. Most of the unrest was centred on the industrial suburb of Kulomzino, which the army first surrounded and then restored to order with such brutality that by the end there were over 1,000 dead, if a British witness is to be believed. However, there was also unrest in the city centre and, gaining control of the prison, the Bolsheviks freed the twenty-seven SR prisoners transferred there from Ufa. Once Kolchak's forces were back in control, the freed prisoners accepted an assurance that they would come to no harm if they returned to prison and most dutifully did so. However there was no trial. On 22 December Cossack troops went on the rampage. They roamed the town, setting homes ablaze, rounding up suspected workers and beating, whipping and killing at will. Among their victims were the SRs who had so meekly returned to their cells. They were subjected to a kangaroo court before being shot. Their mutilated bodies were then dumped on the banks of the river Irtysh. Although reportedly moved to tears by the news of these murders, Kolchak refused a request that there be a thorough investigation of what became known as the Omsk massacre.[4]

Many members of the Czechoslovak Legion found this persecution of the SRs difficult to stomach; they had, after all, fought side by side in the overthrow of the Bolsheviks. Although General Gajda had sided with Kolchak, the Czechoslovak National Council, which represented the army rank and file, was much less enthusiastic. On 21 November it met in Chelyabinsk and advised soldiers not to cooperate with the coup-makers nor to obey orders from pro-Kolchak officers. There were mutinies in December as soldiers committees in parts of the Fifth and Sixth Czechoslovak Regiments, and the entire Seventh Regiment, refused to go to the front. News of the Omsk massacre caused further protests and in January 1919 the Czechoslovak Legion left the front to take up policing duties on the Trans-Siberian Railway.[5]

Although Kolchak's government issued a series of statements about the 'democratic foundation' of the state and its 'support for the rule of law', such declarations were an empty facade. What motivated the White officers, just as much as the desire to crush the Bolsheviks, was the opportunity to take revenge on those felt to be responsible for all Russia's woes; in particular that meant those, essentially the SRs, associated with the Provisional Government of 1917 and its moves to democratize the Russian Army. To cite the definitive history of Kolchak's regime: 'Harking back to the privileges and institutions of the Tsarist past, the officers and atamans of Kolchak's army would exhibit an unquenchable thirst not so much for victory as for revenge upon those who, through revolution, had denied the military caste its cherished place in that dead empire.'[6]

Kolchak's Regime

The nature of Kolchak's regime was quickly established. There was a constitutional fiction: the Council of Ministers, established by the Directory and actually subservient to the Directory, had deposed the Directory and proclaimed a dictatorship – it therefore retained the right to review all laws before passing them to Kolchak to enact. The reality was different. Kolchak could take extraordinary powers without consulting any ministers and increasingly he did just that, relying on the advice of *ad hoc* political groupings and whichever of his ambitious favourites was able to catch his ear. In the opinion of one of his British advisors, Sir Bernard Pares, Kolchak's favourites were 'a mob of adventurers and incompetents'. Understandably, Kolchak saw his main task as winning the war; he would see his Chief-of-Staff two or three times a day and spent two-fifths of his time as Supreme Ruler visiting the front. Thus he rarely attended the Council of Ministers and left much of the administration of his realm in the hands of Mikhailov.

Kolchak's views on the future constitutional form of the Russian state were unclear. He was intolerant of existing democratic institutions since every major regional and city council in Siberia was dominated by the SRs and had protested at his seizure of power. Kolchak's response was to suspend their budgets, only restoring funds to those councils which seemed likely to recognize him after elections were held in April. As to central government, Kolchak had promised that, on the point of victory over the Bolsheviks, he would surrender power, although the assembly envisioned by him would be free of 'idle talkers' and open only to 'healthy elements'. In the interim, however, there was to be no assembly. On assuming power Kolchak had summoned a State Economic Conference. This body, which included his ministers and representatives of private banks, industrialists and Siberia's cooperatives, was the nearest thing to a consultative assembly that Kolchak was prepared to accept. It had two main functions. First and foremost it had a simple duty: to feed and supply the army. However, he also agreed that it could be used as a sounding board for financial and industrial policy. Once summoned, however, even this modest assembly was allowed to atrophy. By May 1919 it had gone into recess, pending a review of its statute. It would only be revived in the dying days of Kolchak's administration.

The powers of the civilian administration were, in any case, severely restricted. Military censorship applied throughout Siberia. All territory west of the river Irtysh was subject to military courts, leaving the civilian government controlling only Tomsk Province and the Trans-Siberian belt from Omsk to Lake Baikal; further east, military rule also applied. When Kolchak's army began to retreat, military control was extended to the whole of Siberia. The army's main concern was manpower. If in 1918 most of those joining the struggle against the Bolsheviks had been volunteers, by the time of the big campaigns of 1919 conscription had become essential for both sides. Recruits to Kolchak's army were taken fresh from the village and given no political training; the Whites were confident that the 'spirit' of Russia and the Russians made this unnecessary. Yet such confidence in the instinctive loyalty of honest Russian peasant was absurd given the recruitment methods used: peasants were taken at gunpoint, poorly fed, and their families, in stark contrast to Red Army practice, were not even offered a pension should they be injured or killed.[7]

Allied, particularly British, military support for Kolchak was crucial. The British Cabinet had agreed on 14 November to support the Directory as an anti-Bolshevik democratic government in Russia. It had done so after much heart-searching, since the First World War had ended on 11 November and the initial support for the Directory had been predicated on the need to have a government in Russia willing to re-open the Eastern Front. However, Bolshevik actions during the Red Terror had convinced the cabinet that there was a humanitarian case for continued intervention. Not only had 10,000 Russians been killed, but in the aftermath of the attempt on Lenin's life on 30 August, the British naval attaché in Petrograd had been killed when Bolshevik security forces raided the British embassy there. At the same time the British representative in Russia, Bruce Lockhart, had been arrested.[8]

The overthrow of the Directory faced the British Cabinet with an acute dilemma. This was compounded by the contradictory advice coming from its political and military advisers in Omsk. Sir Charles Eliot, the British High Commissioner in Siberia, informed the Foreign Office on 29 December 1918 that the new regime was predominantly monarchist and reactionary. It was thoroughly compromised by the violent activities of renegade officers, he reported, and it would always be regarded with distrust by moderate groups and the population as a whole. 'I cannot consider it as a strong government or recommend that we should back it unreservedly,' he concluded.[9] However, although British diplomats had supported the Directory, the military adviser, General Knox, had always respected Kolchak and shared the antipathy of Russian officers towards the SRs in general and Chernov in particular. He had stated unequivocally and in public: 'Siberia is not ready for democracy. What is needed is a dictator. The only question is that of who is the most suitable for the role, General Gajda or Admiral Kolchak.'[10] Although Knox had played no direct role in organizing Kolchak's coup, he welcomed it once it had taken place. British support predominated over that of all other Allies. The Supreme Ruler wore a British greatcoat, was habitually escorted by the Middlesex battalion and was attended by Knox at state banquets where 'God Save the King' would inevitably follow the Russian anthem. Favouring Knox over Eliot, the British Cabinet decided to pursue its intervention strategy.

Support was not limited to military matters. One of Kolchak's closest advisers, meeting him on a daily basis, was the Petrograd financier S.G. Feodosev, at one time State Comptroller in the Tsar's wartime cabinet. By autumn 1918 Feodosev was in charge of the huge Kyshtim, Irtysh and Tanalyk Mining Companies. The chairman of these companies, to whom Feodosev was subordinate, was the Scottish entrepreneur Leslie Urquhart. Responsible through his extensive mining concessions in the Urals and the Altai for much of the old empire's gold production, no less than half its copper production and its entire output of lead and zinc, after the revolution Urquhart had become a staunch advocate of Allied intervention. He had been recruited by the Foreign Office to run the Siberian Supply Company, a Whitehall-funded agency which was intended in the short term to relieve shortages in Siberia through trade, but which had clearly been designed with the longer term aim in mind of securing for Britain as much of a monopoly of Siberian trade as possible. It was Feodosev who was given by Kolchak the task of overseeing the reintroduction of free trade in Siberia.[11]

If trade was to be free in Kolchak's Russia, labour certainly was not. The regime's attitude to labour can be summed up by the fact that the Ministry of Labour was located in a one-room flat in a far-flung Omsk suburb. In January 1919 the old Tsarist system of sickness insurance was reintroduced, excluding as it did all state employees and giving workers only minimal representation in their oversight. No laws defining trade union rights were ever passed by Kolchak, who firmly insisted that, in time of war, strikes were illegal. Unions were obliged to register with the authorities, a time-consuming process, and decree powers were used to close down any trade union engaged in organizing strikes; where martial law operated it was the army which implemented these decrees. There were mass arrests of trade unionists in Omsk in January 1919 but despite such harassment, between 1 January and 1 November 1919 one third of the labour force felt oppressed enough to take part in strike activity. The causes were always the same: low pay, the dismissal of colleagues or long working hours. Siberian employers took the opportunity of the new climate to resurrect the worst aspects of the pre-revolutionary era. In action to suppress a strike on the railways 500 workers were killed by Siberian Cossack forces.[12]

Low pay, however, was a feature of a broader economic crisis, since twelve per cent of factories were closed for lack of fuel. In the last six months of 1919 wages rose by 169% but prices for essential foods were up by 764%. Mikhailov, who was advised by V.N. Kokovtsev, the former Minister of Finance to the Tsar, had planned in spring 1919 that the government would be self-sufficient, except for military expenditure; however, by July 1919 monthly expenditure was twice the budget figure, with sufficient income to cover only one eighth of expenditure. At the same time Mikhailov tried to introduce a currency reform which would withdraw all the old Kerensky money and allow trade to take place only in the

Siberian rouble established in January 1919; the population, however, simply refused to surrender the old notes. Fuel of all sorts was in desperately short supply and extremely expensive. Although the Urals was a coal-producing area, there was not enough coal produced locally for the needs of the railway and much of the coking coal needed for metal working had traditionally been transported from the Donets Basin in southern Russia and was no longer available. Nearly half the goods moved on the Tomsk section of the Trans-Siberian Railway was coal needed for the railway system itself, which provided a regular eight-day long service from Omsk to the Pacific.[13]

The only aspect of the economy to flourish was agriculture, but this caused political complications. The First World War had seen a rapid growth in the activity of Siberian cooperatives, boosted by contracts to supply the Imperial Army. These cooperatives had become increasingly mechanized and large scale, concentrating on dairy products and the grain trade. However, their management committees were dominated by SR sympathizers, albeit the more conservative ones. They were therefore hostile to Kolchak, just as he was antagonistic towards them. Meeting in Omsk just before Kolchak's coup, the liberal All-Russian Congress of Trade and Industry had described the cooperatives as 'internal Bolshevism' and Kolchak shared this view; the Fourth All-Siberian Cooperative Congress planned for July 1919 was banned. This antagonism between Kolchak and the peasantry meant that grain supplies were always a problem, and Kolchak resorted to the traditional if unimaginative policy of forced grain requisitioning at fixed prices.[14]

When it came to the future of the land itself, Kolchak promised much but gave little. Back on 6 July 1918 as one of its first acts Mikhailov's Siberian Government had passed a law ordering land to be returned to its former owners pending the summoning of a new Constituent Assembly. This was essentially a declaration of principle, since the vast majority of Siberian peasants were settlers who had neither been serfs nor former serfs and had never had to live alongside a landed aristocracy. The issue, therefore, was not land policy in Siberia but whether this law would be enforced in the rest of Russia when Kolchak's forces moved from Siberia into the Russian heartland, particularly the Volga area where landlordism had always been an issue and peasants had received land in February 1918 from the Bolshevik-Left SR coalition government.

Kolchak was uncertain what to do. On 16 February 1919 he made a strongly worded if vague pro-peasant speech at a meeting in Ekaterinburg, but there were no immediate changes. Then on 5 April 1919 his Council of Ministers repealed the law of 6 July 1918 and made clear that those peasants who had acquired land would be allowed to retain it temporarily and harvest it in 1919; no further land seizures would be permitted, but Kolchak did promise he would 'take measures to provide in the future for the landless peasants... utilizing first of all the land of private owners and of the state'. Although Kolchak insisted that only his planned National Assembly could finally resolve the land question, his government did promise 'to make available wide opportunities for acquiring full property rights' of land which had been temporarily acquired; in other words, peasants would be able to buy the land they had been given. On 13 April 1919, as a move to facilitate this, Kolchak brought all land acquired by the peasants under state control and arranged for it to be rented out to them. The clear implication of both these moves was that peasants would have to pay for any land they gained, and that the subsequent funds acquired by the state could be used to compensate the former owners. However, when the details of this scheme were discussed by the Council of Ministers, it was defeated by conservative groups and all talk of land reform was put in abeyance. Kolchak's proposals, with their insistence that all land had to be paid for, were reminiscent of the Stolypin reforms introduced after the 1905 revolution and were a far cry from the simple Bolshevik promise of November 1917.[15]

Red-Green Agreement?

Given the reactionary nature of the Kolchak regime and its vicious assault on the leadership of the SR Party, some sort of accommodation between the SR and Bolshevik leaders was a logical development. In Siberia it was a desire shared by both sides. Harking back to the brief period of cooperation among soviet parties in September 1917 when resisting General Kornilov's attempted coup, Siberian communists wrote to Lenin making the following plea: 'all workers and revolutionaries who remain alive, and all those supporters of the republic, express only one wish – the speediest possible conclusion of an agreement with the socialists and pro-republic groupings on the platform of political compromise; "Power to the People!", because if the hostility between the soviets and these groupings continues, it would end with the destruction of the working class.'[16] Motivated by similar concerns Volskii, a member of the SR Central Committee, leader of the SR delegation to the Ufa State Conference and the leading survivor of the Komuch administration, decided to seek an agreement with the Bolsheviks. Volskii did not come empty handed. On the eve of Kolchak's coup the SRs had established significant volunteer military units loyal to the Constituent Assembly; the possibility that these forces might join the Red Army, or at the very least remain neutral as the Red Army approached Ufa, gave Volskii an important bargaining chip.

At a meeting held in Ufa on 5 December 1918 surviving members of the SR Central Committee voted to change the party's stance towards the Bolsheviks. All military action against the Red Army would cease. As a result, even before the Red Army took Ufa on 30 December, contacts between the two parties had begun. Initially these contacts were between local leaders of the Bolshevik and SR Party organizations, both forced by Kolchak to operate underground. They agreed on how the Red Army and Constituent Assembly volunteers would cooperate in liberating Ufa. However, once the city was taken, the nature of the talks changed considerably. The SR representatives, the Ufa Delegation as it

A Red Army armoured car at a Moscow training base, 1918.

became known, persuaded the local Bolsheviks that the talks were no longer taking place between two parties but between representatives of Lenin's Soviet Government and the (albeit temporarily overthrown) Komuch Government responsible to the Constituent Assembly. In Moscow Lenin was not happy with this interpretation of the talks, but to help move things along it was agreed to annul the decree of 14 June which had expelled the SRs, as well as the Mensheviks, from the soviets. Formal discussions started in Ufa on 31 December and proceeded slowly. The sticking point was the SRs' insistence on raising the fate of the Constituent Assembly; they called for the formation of a government responsible to the Constituent Assembly, something Lenin could never concede.

Not all SRs were happy with Volskii's initiative. Although party leader Chernov did not at first dissociate himself from Volskii's move, he had used his last address to Constituent Assembly deputies on 28 November 1918 to suggest a rather different strategy: assuming a satisfactory agreement could not be reached with the Bolsheviks about forming a government responsible to the Constituent Assembly, the SR Party should break off the talks and prepare for a struggle against both Bolsheviks and Whites, he had said. Volskii felt an agreement with the Bolsheviks was still possible, however, and the talks moved from Ufa to Moscow. There, to resolve the disagreement between the Chernov and Volskii factions, the Bolsheviks allowed the SR Party to hold a conference in early February 1919. The resulting resolution was both good and bad news for those seeking compromise. The conference condemned the Whites and their foreign backers, and resolved to oppose all attempts at restoration; the party therefore reaffirmed its commitment to ending the military struggle against the Bolsheviks. However, the conference went on to condemn Volskii and the Ufa Delegation for apparently being ready to make concessions on the issue of the Constituent Assembly; the delegation was instructed to abstain from any negotiation with the soviet authorities concerning a political agreement.

Despite the conference resolution, Volskii and his Ufa Delegation continued to negotiate at talks held from 9-19 February 1919. The Bolshevik side was led by Kamenev, that long-time advocate of a socialist coalition government. The main issue to be addressed was that of legalizing the SR Party. After spending ten days trying to tie the SRs to a commitment which would link their relegalization to a promise not to criticize the soviet authorities, the Bolsheviks backed down and agreed to legalize the party unconditionally. This enhanced the status of the Ufa Delegation and rather embarrassed Chernov and the SR Central Committee, which put out a statement making clear that the Ufa Delegation was a group composed of surviving deputies to the Constituent Assembly who had no formal status within the SR Party; the SR Central Committee had not taken part in the legalization negotiations.[17]

These talks with the SRs were only part of a more general Bolshevik policy of reconciliation launched at the end of 1918 and continuing for the first two months of 1919. Not only were the SRs allowed back into the soviets, so too were the Mensheviks. On 22 January 1919 the Menshevik paper *Vsegda Vpered* was published legally for the first time since the summer of 1918 and quickly attracted a circulation of over 100,000. The launch of the paper coincided with the Second Congress of Trade Unions, at which there was a vociferous group of Menshevik deputies who demanded genuine trade union freedom. Coincidentally or not, renewed activity by the Mensheviks was followed by a rash of strikes in the two capitals Moscow and Petrograd, and such provincial centres as Tula, Bryansk, Tver and Sormovo, the latter a traditional base for the SR Party. Mensheviks certainly played a role in organizing these strikes. The Cheka clearly thought it a major role...[18]

Early 1919 also saw a debate about the role of the Cheka. Its reputation for arbitrary cruelty during the Red Terror was well deserved, and if the other socialist parties were to be brought back into the political life of the soviets its role would have to change. On 9 January 1919 Kamenev, who had campaigned for limitations on the powers of the Cheka for some time, actually proposed that it be abolished. This was not supported, but at the end of January the Moscow Party organization called for the Cheka's powers to be limited to investigation, depriving it of the power to act as investigator, judge and executioner. At the same time delegates to the Second Congress of Trade Unions were told by a leading Bolshevik that the Cheka had behaved 'pretty stupidly' when it had intervened to settle industrial disputes. When a decision was finally taken on 17

February the reforms in the Cheka were not as radical as many had hoped. At district level where local tyrants had often held sway it was abolished completely, while elsewhere its powers were defined essentially as investigation. However, Lenin insisted the institution itself could not be abolished. It was essential, he felt, to correct mistakes and remove excesses, rather than fundamentally changing its methods of operation. The limits of the reform were seen at once: on 22 February *Vsegda Vpered* was closed down by the Cheka and leading Mensheviks arrested.[19]

The legalization of the SR Party was similarly circumscribed. The SR paper *Delo naroda*, which reappeared on 20 March 1919, was soon in trouble. It was very critical of the Bolshevik regime, more outspoken even than *Vsegda Vpered*, having no hesitation in publishing material on the Red Terror and the atrocities of the Cheka. In its first issue it published one of the resolutions adopted at the SRs' February Conference which concluded: 'we demand that the ruling party abolish the dictatorship of the party, abandon the policy of violence in the countryside, and re-establish all civil liberties, generally and during elections to the soviets in particular'. After ten issues, during which time the paper also achieved a circulation of 100,000, it was closed down.[20] The Cheka persuaded the Moscow Soviet that, legal or not, parties which made such statements were 'counter-revolutionary'. What the term 'counter-revolutionary' actually meant was this: in the Moscow Soviet elections held early in 1919, candidates standing for the Menshevik and SR Parties had done exceptionally well; in Petrograd the Left SRs posed a similar threat to the Bolsheviks. Without the interventions of the Cheka there was a constant danger that the SRs, once back in the soviets, might succeed in winning control of them and thus depriving the Bolsheviks of power.

Lenin and the Peasants

The hesitant, and ultimately rather limited reconciliation between the Bolsheviks and the SRs came in the context of Lenin's own extremely tentative reassessment of his peasant policy. Over the winter of 1918-19 he began to reconsider his attitude to what he called the petty-bourgeoisie, in other words, the peasants and their political representatives. This was a gradual process which began with an article published in *Pravda* on 21 November 1918 entitled *The Valuable Admissions of Pitirim Sorokin*. Sorokin had been an active member of both the SR Party and the URR, a deputy to the Constituent Assembly and one of those involved in helping stage an insurrection in Archangel at the moment of the British landing. But *Pravda* of 21 November published an open letter from him in which he declared he was leaving the SR Party and relinquishing his seat in the Constituent Assembly (he subsequently emigrated to the United States and pursued a successful academic career). For Lenin it was the first real sign of what he felt would become a trend among petty-bourgeois democrats pushing them away from hostility towards the Bolsheviks and towards neutrality towards them. The Kolchak coup and the British support for it had brought about this change, which could be linked to the question of patriotism. He wrote:

> Patriotism is one of the most deeply ingrained sentiments, inculcated by the existence of separate fatherlands for hundreds of thousands of years. One of the most pronounced, one might say exceptional difficulties of our proletarian revolution is that it was obliged to pass through a phase of extreme departure from patriotism, the phase of the Brest-Litovsk Peace. The bitterness, resentment, and violent indignation provoked by this peace was easy to understand and it goes without saying that we Marxists could expect only the class conscious proletariat to appreciate the truth that we were making and were obliged to make great national sacrifices for the sake of the supreme interests of the world proletarian revolution... At best our tactics appeared [to non-Marxists] a fantastic, fanatical and adventurist sacrifice of the real... for the sake of an abstract, utopian and dubious hope...But it has turned out as we had said....
>
> The objective conditions which repelled these democratic patriots from us most strongly have now vanished. The objective conditions existing in the world now compel them to turn to us. Pitirim Sorokin's change of front is by no means fortuitous, but rather the symptom of an inevitable change of front on the part of a whole class of the petty-bourgeois democracy. Whoever fails to reckon with this fact and to take advantage of it is a bad socialist, not a Marxist...
>
> A split among them is inevitable: one section will come over to our side, another section will remain neutral, while a third will deliberately join forces with the monarchist Constitutional Democrats [liberals], who are selling Russia to Anglo-American capital and seeking to crush the revolution with the aid of foreign bayonets. One of the most urgent tasks of the present day is to take into account and make use of the turn among the Mensheviks and Socialist Revolutionary democrats from hostility to Bolshevism first to neutrality and then to support of Bolshevism...It would be foolish to insist on tactics of suppression and terror in relation to petty-bourgeois democrats when the course of events is compelling them to turn in our direction.

Here, then, was the justification for the semi-reconciliation of early 1919, and, having dealt with the political leaders, Lenin then began to think about their supporters, the peasants. He continued:

Our task in the rural areas is to destroy the landowner and smash the resistance of the exploiter and the kulak profiteer. For this purpose we can safely rely only on the semi-proletarians, the 'poor peasants'. But the middle peasant is not our enemy. He wavered, is wavering and will continue to waver. The task of influencing the waverers is not identical with the task of overthrowing the exploiter and defeating the active enemy. The task at the moment is to come to an agreement with the middle peasant...[21]

This was the first time Lenin had even hinted at the notion that the Poor Peasants' Committees had been a mistake and that the middle peasant could be an alternative source of support for the Bolsheviks. Support for the middle peasant would become a new orthodoxy by spring 1919, but for now Lenin was still essentially thinking out loud. At an address to a meeting of Moscow Party workers on 27 November he developed a similar theme. This time, however, he reinforced his points by rooting them firmly in the writings of Engels. Quoting *The Peasant Question in France and Germany*, Lenin noted that Engels had written:

When we are in possession of state power we shall not even think of forcibly expropriating the small peasants... Our task consists... in effecting a transition of his private enterprise and private possession to cooperative ones, not forcibly but by dint of example and the proffer of social assistance for this purpose.

In the Russian context, Lenin went on, this meant: 'for the middle peasant we say – no force under any circumstance; for the big peasant we say – our aim is to bring him under the control of the grain monopoly and fight him when he violates the monopoly and conceals grain.' Unfortunately, Lenin went on: 'In our party literature, as in our propaganda and agitation, we have always stressed the distinction between our attitude to the big bourgeoisie and the petty bourgeoisie. But although we are all in agreement as to theory, not all of us by a long shot have drawn the correct political conclusions.' He concluded: 'so the tactics we have been pursuing for six months must be modified to suit the new tasks with regard to the various groups of petty bourgeois democrats.'[22]

This new interest in the middle peasant was far from being consistently expressed, even by Lenin. Addressing the Soviet on 22 October he had made no mention of the middle peasant and argued that, with the support of the poor peasants, the October Revolution was now moving into the villages and every village 'can proceed to lay the foundations of a new socialist Russia'.[23] Addressing the Sixth Congress of Soviets in the first week of November 1918 he had defended the creation of the Poor Peasant Committees and went on:

We have now reached a point where the socialist revolution in the rural areas has begun... And so the countryside, the rural poor, uniting with their leaders, the city workers, are only now providing us with a firm and stable foundation for real socialist construction. Socialist construction will only now begin in the countryside. Only now are Soviets and farms being formed which are systematically working towards large-scale socialized farming...[24]

Addressing Poor Peasants' Committees on 8 November he promised one thousand million roubles to form and develop communes adding: 'division of the land was all very well as a beginning.... but that is not enough. The solution lies in socialized farming.'[25] Talk of socialized farming was the polar opposite of support for the middle peasants.

These comments were made before the change of heart of Pitirim Sorokin, but even after that Lenin continued to praise the wonders of socialist farming. On 11 December 1918 Lenin addressed the First All-Russian Congress of Land Departments, Poor Peasants' Committees and Communes and his speech was published in *Pravda* on 14 December. In this speech Lenin pointed out how the agrarian revolution had never got beyond its first stage: the aristocratic land-lord had been overthrown, but the revolution 'still had not touched the more powerful and more modern enemy of all working people, capital'. He then portrayed the SR insurrections of summer 1918 as 'kulak' inspired, and depicted the establishment of the Poor Peasants' Committees as the Bolshevik response to the capitalist agriculture of the kulaks. He went on 'the great agrarian revolution would inevitably have remained a paper revolution if the urban workers had not stirred into action the rural proletariat... Socialist construction depends entirely on this step.'

Naturally, Lenin warned that this could not happen over night, but, with the beginnings of world revolution clearly being discernible 'it is impossible to live in the old way... The productivity of labour could be doubled or tripled if a transition were made from scattered small-scale farming to collective farming'. Lenin added that 'the poor peasants did not take the land from the landowners for it to fall into the hands of the kulaks', and that the February 1918 Land Reform Law had always envisaged 'the aim to develop collective farming'. While he repeated the notion that Bolshevik policy remained to 'form an alliance with the middle peasantry', such an alliance could only be forged through example and therefore 'it is for this purpose, for collective farming, that the communes and state farms are being formed'.[26] Just three days later, however, Lenin told workers in the Presnya district of Moscow 'if a local soviet somewhere or other hits the middle peasant hard and it hurts, that soviet must be taken away because it does not know how to act properly.'[27] Thereafter Lenin became involved in resolving a series of incidents where the Soviet authorities had gratuitously antagonized 'middle peasants'. On 16 December it was the overzealous behaviour of the Poor Peasants' Committee in Budilov village, Yaroslavl province; later in December he learned that the chairman of a Poor Peasants' Committee in Tver province was a former Tsarist gendarme, while a local soviet in Vologda province was discovered to have excluded middle peasants from the voters' lists in local elections.[28]

Bolshevik policy towards the peasantry was thus extraordinarily confused in the autumn and winter of 1918-19. The establishment of Poor Peasants' Committees to enforce grain requisitioning and root out alleged kulak grain hoarders had proved counter-productive. In the second half of 1918 the Cheka recorded 100 peasant rebellions; according to reports in the Menshevik press peasant rebellions took place in Tver, Yaroslavl, Kostroma, Vladimir, Vitebsk, Kazan, Tula, Voronezh, Ryazan, Kaluga, Smolensk and Tambov provinces at the end of 1918.[29] No wonder a decree abolishing the Poor Peasants' Committees was quietly signed on 4 December 1918. Yet despite all the attempts to woo the middle peasant, the ultimate aim of socialist agriculture was never abandoned. On 14 February 1919 regulations on socialist land measures were introduced in Moscow; these declared that all agriculture based on peasant family farms was 'transitional and obsolescent' and called for the development of state and collective farms.[30]

Kolchak advances and retreats

The confused Bolshevik policy towards the SR Party and the peasants was reflected on the battlefield. The new tolerance towards the SR Party had enabled the Red Army to capture Ufa at the end of December; yet a week earlier they had lost control of Perm because the activities of the Poor Peasants' Committees there had undermined their popular base. The attitude of the local peasantry was the central feature of all the fighting during Russia's civil war, and explains how it was that Kolchak could advance so dramatically in his first campaign, and then was forced into a steady retreat.

Once Kolchak had consolidated his hold on power, work resumed on the long delayed advance westwards along the Trans-Siberian Railway through Perm to Vyatka and the anticipated rendezvous with British forces descending via the river Dvina and the Kotlas railway from Archangel. The advance began in mid-December and on 24-5 December 1918 Kolchak's forces, commanded by General Gajda, defeated the Third Red Army and captured Perm. It was a great victory, although marred by the brutal murder of 1,500 workers accused of Bolshevism.[31] Characteristically, the capture of Perm was far from being a purely military affair. Stalin was sent to investigate why this strategically sensitive city had fallen, and discovered that the Red Army had been forced to fight on two fronts, not only against the White Army but 'against elusive inhabitants in the rear who, under the direction of White-guard agents, blew up railway tracks and created all sorts of difficulties'. Although Stalin could not bring himself to admit that the Poor Peasants' Committees were a failure, he did recognize that it was these committees 'controlled by kulaks' which had taken a lead 'in uniting the countryside against Soviet power'. If Poor Peasants'

A White guard post on the Trans-Siberian railway, winter of 1918-19.

Committees really were in the hands of the kulaks, logic suggested that the whole village was opposed to Bolshevik policy.[32]

Kolchak's army waited in Perm for the weather to improve and for its reserves to accumulate before resuming the advance in the spring. The timing of this renewed offensive became a source of some controversy between Kolchak and his various advisers. Although Perm had fallen, the situation on the Eastern Front was not all that Kolchak would have wished. His western march along the Trans-Siberian had not been matched by forces deployed further south. Not only had the Red Army captured Ufa, but by the end of January Uralsk and Orenburg were also in Bolshevik hands. More importantly perhaps, although the Third Red Army had been forced to abandon Perm, it had retreated in relatively good order. For these reasons, in debates held during January and February 1919 some of Kolchak's more experienced commanders, supported by the British adviser General Knox, argued that it would be wise to delay any further operations for a few months until the Russian Army was fully trained, organized and equipped, and until a strategic reserve could be forged. However, Kolchak preferred to listen to the advice of his young Chief-of-Staff Major-General D.A. Lebedev, who argued for a rapid return to the offensive while, as he saw it, the 'Reds' were unprepared. Lebedev began his offensive on 3 March without informing Knox. Despite all Knox's warnings that an army was only as strong as its reserves, there was no reserve as the offensive began.[33]

Initially, all went according to plan. In the north General Gajda advanced west along the Trans-Siberian from Perm towards Vyatka for some 100 miles meeting stubborn resistance. Further south General M.V. Khanzhin advanced towards Ufa. Here he met little resistance and was able to advance at great speed, capturing Ufa and moving further west. The speed of Khanzhin's advance needs some explanation. Khanzhin's forces contained the remnants of what in 1918 had been the Directory's People's Army. Most of them had been recruited in summer 1918 from regions under Komuch administration, such as the Volga and Kama river basins. These, then, were soldiers who were returning home. They were also returning to an area where the SRs were traditionally strong, and where the Bolsheviks' policy of establishing Poor Peasants' Committees had been extremely unpopular. When the Izhevsk area was freed of Bolshevik control, it was alleged that some 7,000 people had been executed during an outburst of Red terror. As Khanzhin's forces advanced in March and April there were peasant insurrections in nearby Syzran, Simbirsk and Samara. Unrest affected 100,000 to 150,000 peasants.[34]

Kolchak's victory was short-lived. The reactionary nature of his regime and the timidity of his statements on land reform in April meant that disillusionment was rapid. Equally, Lenin's growing interest in the middle peasant and his willingness to strike a deal of sorts with the SRs helped to change the popular mood. The Red Army was soon able to counter-attack and when its advance began it was dramatic. During April Red Army forces on the Eastern Front were trebled and by early May the Red Army had made Khanzhin retreat in order to prevent his lines becoming over-extended; by early June Khanzhin had once again lost control of Ufa, retreating to the line from which Kolchak's spring offensive had started. This retreat exposed Gajda's flank further north on the Trans-Siberian Railway. By the start of June, after a slow but steady advance, he had reached Glazov, nearly two thirds of the way from Perm to Vyatka; by mid-June he had been forced to retreat back to Perm. In a desperate gamble to stem the tide, Kolchak committed to battle the Volga Corps of General Kappel, the only reserves he had accumulated. This corps, however, had also been formed from units which had begun life as part of the People's Army; 10,000 of them deserted at once, joining the many other unwilling conscripts who abandoned the cause in droves.[35]

Desertions on this scale did not give troops to the Red Army, however, but to Green partisans fighting behind Kolchak's lines. The first anti-White peasant uprisings in Siberia had begun even before Kolchak came to power when the then Siberian Government began its policy of grain seizures and enforced conscription. By the end of November 1918 the first partisans groups had established a military HQ in a village to the south and east of Krasnoyarsk, and by December 1918 groups such as these had captured Minusinsk and Krasnoyarsk itself which they held for a short period. Although this insurrection was put down by the end of January, it reignited only a week later and continued into March. The March unrest was even more widespread and extended to

Kustanaiskii and Tyumen Provinces. Thus even before Kolchak's advance began, there was serious unrest in his rear.[36] As the advance proper began, so the Green movement intensified, fuelled by growing disillusionment with Kolchak. A sympathetic correspondent noted the change of mood by the summer: 'temporary sympathy to the Whites was quickly extinguished by the spilled blood of peasants during pacification campaigns, requisitions and robberies. The masses who only recently celebrated liberation [from the Bolsheviks] are now getting ready for the overthrow of the new ruler.' Peasant rebellion was soon an endemic problem for Kolchak. Conservative estimates put the number of Green forces at 100,000. Kolchak's response only made the situation worse: punitive expeditions, the taking of hostages, the burning of homesteads, the literal decimation of villages where 'bandits' were not handed over, such policies could only backfire.[37]

Forced to retreat, Kolchak had no choice but to seek to broaden his support base. In particular, he targeted the most conservative representatives of SR opinion, the cooperative leaders. As part of a whole series of initiatives, in May 1919 the State Economic Conference was revived and its statute modified to give increased representation to the cooperatives, as well as representatives from regional and town councils. Kolchak stated that in future all legislation would be scrutinized by the conference and some politicians in Kolchak's domain appeared to believe that a new preparliament was about to be born. The State Economic Conference opened in Omsk in June with great ceremony, and some right-wing SRs did indeed appear willing to play the role of a loyal opposition. After drawing up a list of complaints, the new assembly sent a delegation in person to Kolchak which he, with some hesitation, agreed to receive. As a result a Committee for the Defence of Public Order was established which had the power to countermand any illegal decision taken by the military authorities. However, when at the end of August 1919 the State Economic Conference tried to revise its statutes once more and give itself more powers, Kolchak refused to have anything more to do with it. At this point the right-wing SRs returned to being a disloyal opposition and Kolchak resumed the role of dictator.[38]

By July 1919, then, Kolchak's regime was in crisis. On 1 July Perm was surrendered to the Red Army. Thus ended the dream of a rendezvous with British forces from Archangel. By mid-July Ekaterinburg had fallen with the result that all the mines, factories and railways of the Urals region were in Bolshevik hands. By 2 August Chelyabinsk was also back in Bolshevik hands. Meeting from 26 July to 20 August Allied representatives, gathered under the auspices of the Omsk Diplomatic Conference, concluded that Kolchak was a lost cause. London once again took the lead. On 29 July it was announced in the House of Commons that, given the impossibility of capturing Kotlas, Archangel would be abandoned. Then, on 5 August, Knox relayed to Kolchak that henceforth all British aid was being concentrated in southern Russia in the hands of General Denikin.

Securing the Don

The British decision to move its focus of attention from Kolchak in Siberia to the Don area of southern Russia could not have been taken any earlier for, although it would be Denikin's forces which ultimately came closest to defeating the Bolsheviks, for much of 1919 they were confined to the Kuban, where they had first been driven by Antonov-Ovseenko and Muraviev in February 1918. Although the vicissitudes of the First World War and its aftermath had kept the flame of counter-revolution alive in South Russia, the real enemy as far as the Bolsheviks were concerned remained Kolchak. The German occupation of Ukraine in 1918 had enabled the Whites to survive the Red onslaught of that spring; they were thus able to pose a continued threat to the Bolshevik regime into the winter of 1918-19. However, by spring 1919 Trotsky's Red Army had restored soviet power to the Don and the White forces still found themselves pinned down on the fringe of Russia.

In May 1918 the German occupying forces in Ukraine took control of Rostov on Don. This gave a new lease of life to the local White forces. The Kuban could be reached from the Russian heartland either via the railway through Rostov on Don, or, further east, along the Tsaritsyn railway. The German occupation of Rostov on Don meant fighting against the Reds could be concentrated on the Tsaritsyn exit route. By May 1918 the Volunteer Army established by Kornilov was not the only anti-Bolshevik force in the field. Anti-Bolshevik Cossacks, supported and armed by the German administration, took control of their capital Novocherkassk on 6 May and gradually extended their control until by mid-June they number 40,000 men with 56 field guns and 179 machine guns. At a session of their traditional assembly, the Great Krug, which lasted from late August to early October, they elected as their new ataman General Krasnov, the man who had collaborated in Kornilov's coup attempt and had tried to overthrow the Bolsheviks at Pulkovo Heights just days after the successful seizure of power. Krasnov sent his forces to capture the strategic Volga city of Tsaritsyn which Stalin had been sent to defend. The first major attack was launched in August, and a bigger one in September. A third attack in October very nearly succeeded: the Don Cossacks surrounded the city and there was fighting in the outskirts, before Red reinforcements arrived in the nick of time, having surprised the Cossacks by marching at night for 500 miles to avoid Cossack patrols. The Red Army retained control of Tsaritsyn because it had the advantage in terms of artillery: its men numbered 40,000, the same as the Cossacks, but they had 240 field guns, far more than Krasnov's Cossacks. Nevertheless Stalin claimed much of the credit for organizing the successful defence of this important railway centre which had become home to the armaments and oil industries.

Meanwhile in southern Kuban, similarly protected from the Bolsheviks not only by the German Army but by the Don Cossacks as well, the Volunteer Army was able to recover from the horrors of the Ice March. General Denikin, one of

Kornilov's original co-conspirators, took over command after the latter's death and on 22 June he launched what the volunteers knew as their Second Kuban Campaign. By 19 August the regional capital of Ekaterinodar had finally been captured and by 18 November one of Denikin's ablest commanders General P.N. Wrangel had taken Stavropol. This was an extraordinary campaign in many ways, because Denikin started off with only 9,000 men, supported by 21 field guns and two armoured cars, while in the North Caucasus area there were about ten times that number of men and a vast quantity of equipment nominally loyal to the Soviet Government and formally part of the Red Army. However, these forces were isolated from Soviet Russia proper, and at least one army was led by a Left SR who in October 1918 mirrored the action of Muraviev and rebelled against the Bolsheviks from his base in Pyatigorsk. By September 1918 the Volunteer Army numbered nearly 40,000. This fighting posed little immediate threat to the Bolshevik Government, but it did allow the Whites to establish a territorial base, and a base which, since the capture of Novorossiisk on 26 August, gave the Volunteer Army a Black Sea port through which British aid would later be channelled. During the course of 1919, 198,000 rifles, 62,000 machine guns and 500 million rounds of small arms ammunition would be sent to Denikin's soldiers from Britain. Heavy equipment included 1,121 artillery pieces, 1,900,000 shells, 60 tanks and 168 aircraft.[39]

While the First World War was still being fought, the Black Sea was closed to Allied shipping, but the defeat of Turkey and Bulgaria changed that. Although the Kuban was isolated from central Russia, it could be readily supplied through the Black Sea. For a while, then, the Southern Front seemed an even greater threat to the Bolsheviks than that posed by Kolchak on the Eastern Front. Kolchak's coup initially dislocated the counter-offensive launched by the Directory and postponed serious military operations until the capture of Perm at the end of December. So in November 1918 Trotsky announced that the Southern Front was now a greater danger to the survival of the soviet regime and his command train sped south. During the night of 26-27 November that train received a telegram which read in part:

> On 23 November about 3 p.m. the English light cruiser *Liverpool* and the French cruiser *Ernest Renan* and two destroyers came into Novorossiisk. The representatives who arrived... declared that they would furnish all possible means to restore a united Russia.

The telegram went on to describe how millions of rifle cartridges, thousands of rifles and a quantity of shells had been unloaded, along with some New Zealand troops.[40]

Yet the southern threat was more apparent than real. The end of the First World War not only opened up the Black Sea to Allied shipping, but opened up the whole of Southern Russia to Bolshevik advance. The Germans had been forced to withdraw from Rostov, and, with their departure, a whole new front

A British tank at the point of capture, still bearing the legend 'For Holy Russia'.

could be opened up, enabling the Red Army to attack the rear of the Don Cossack forces whose advance guard was still concentrated away to the east near Tsaritsyn; in December 1918 and again in January 1919 Tsaritsyn had been surrounded by the Cossacks and seemed on the brink of surrender. In a brilliantly successful campaign launched at the end of January 1919 the Red Army quickly regained control of the Don. The Cossack army had risen to 50,000 by November 1918, but fell to 15,000 by February 1919. Whole regiments surrendered to the Bolsheviks, or simply went home tired of fighting just as they had done after the fighting at Pulkovo Heights. In a couple of weeks everything Krasnov had achieved in the previous six months was destroyed.

Up until January 1919 Krasnov's Don Cossacks and Denikin's Volunteer Army had operated as separate entities. Denikin and Krasnov had held talks back at the end of May 1918 about merging their forces but failed to agree since Krasnov had no choice but to cooperate with the Germans, whereas Denikin was fiercely pro-Ally. The end of the First World War and the Red advance into the Don changed all that. On 8 January 1919 the two forces agreed to operational unity, appointing Denikin as Commander-in-Chief, whilst on 15 February Krasnov resigned as ataman. The whole counter-revolutionary movement in the South was now directed from Denikin's headquarters in Ekaterinodar. Such unity clearly gave the White movement much potential strength, but it was still just potential strength. In January 1919 Denikin had planned to move to Tsaritsyn, capture it and then advance in the direction of

Kolchak's forces. The Red advance into the Don meant he was forced to move away from any rendezvous with other White forces and think defensively, concentrating on the North-west of the Kuban and the need to prevent the Red Army penetrating his heartland from the recently reconquered Don. General Z. Mai-Maevskii faced odds of more than three to one as he attempted to keep the Thirteenth Red Army tied down in the Donbas and away from the Kuban. In these circumstances there was no possibility of forging a link with Kolchak and the White danger from the south seemed a thing of the past. In March 1919 Denikin posed little threat to the Bolshevik regime.[41]

World Revolution

If it had been confined to the Eastern Front the Russian civil war would have been over by summer 1919. Denikin was trapped in the Kuban. In April the Red Army staged a successful counter-attack and by May 1919, supported by Green insurgents, it had Kolchak on the run. The February agreement between the Bolsheviks and the Ufa Delegation of SRs seemed to have born fruit. Yet in February 1919 at the same time as the Bolsheviks were reaching the political accord with the SRs which would help them win the war in the east, they were igniting a new civil war in the south and west which would radically change the prospects for the survival of the Bolshevik regime. The defeat of Germany in the First World War and the subsequent retreat of most of its forces from those areas either occupied during the fighting or annexed under the terms of the Treaty of Brest Litovsk created a power vacuum into which the Bolsheviks could step, for behind them the Germans left only the most ephemeral of nationalist movements. World revolution was suddenly back at the top of the Bolsheviks' agenda. Leading figures in the campaigns to establish soviet governments in Latvia and Ukraine respectively, Peteris Stuchka and Vladimir Antonov-Ovseenko, made clear in their memoirs that world revolution was very much on their mind as the Red Army moved westward. For the Latvian Red Army, as it descended the Baltic coast, German East Prussia was only a stone's throw away, while the Ukrainian Red Army stood poised in April 1919 to march to the aid of the Hungarian Soviet Republic which had just been declared.

This process began with the return home of the Latvian Riflemen who had played such a significant role in the first months of the civil war. On 16 November they were ordered to withdraw from Siberia and to prepare to assemble on the Latvian border. This took time, and on 18 November 'bourgeois' nationalists in Riga, with the support of German troops in the city and a British naval ship off shore, proclaimed Latvia's independence. Three weeks later, on 4 December, Latvia's communists announced the formation of a rival Soviet Latvia, and the Latvian Riflemen crossed the frontier. There was little resistance, for by and large the returning riflemen were welcomed. The remnants of the German Army were in no position to fight in any serious way.

Red Latvian Riflemen resting after their return home, spring 1919.

The German garrison at Dorpat (Tartu), some 4,000 strong, simply retreated towards Riga as the Riflemen approached; the same happened at Valk. As the troops approached Riga an insurrection broke out on the night of 2-3 January and by 4 January the capital had been taken. As the Red Army advanced the German soldiers' councils were given to understand that if they retreated steadily the Red Army would follow ten kilometres behind and feel under no obligation actually to attack them. On 13 January the First Congress of Latvian Soviets took place and the Latvian Soviet Socialist Republic was established.[42]

The Red Army's advance into Ukraine was equally rapid. As in Latvia, in winter 1919 the Red Army forces were by and large seen as liberators. As the Germans prepared to withdraw from Ukraine, the Bolsheviks had to decide whether they would collaborate with the nationalist groups which were opposed to the crumbling German-sponsored dictatorship of Hetman Skoropadskii. These nationalists had established a Directory on 13 November 1918, in imitation of that established in Omsk, and succeeded in deposing Skoropadskii on 14 December. Although the Bolsheviks had initially agreed to cooperate with these forces, they changed their mind and launched their own military campaign. On 12 November a small group of communists, including Antonov-Ovseenko and Stalin, moved to Kursk where they established a Provisional Ukrainian Soviet Government on 20 November; from there they launched an assault on the nationalists one month later. Not much more than a fortnight after the nationalists had deposed Skoropadskii, the Red Army defeated the nationalists and entered Kiev on 5 February 1919.

Such a rapid Bolshevik advance was facilitated by the fact that the nationalist Directory was split on the question of land. Although its political leader was committed to radical land reform, its military commander had dictatorial ambitions of his own for himself and favoured an alliance with the middle classes rather than pandering to the land hunger of the peasants. As a result the Directory at first made no statement on land policy and then cobbled together a compromise which promised to expropriate large state and private land holdings, but was very vague about how such land subsequently would be distributed and what impact this might have on existing peasant households. Such confusion split the Directory and persuaded a majority of Ukrainian SRs to support the Bolsheviks in establishing a soviet state; meeting in January 1919 to ratify this decision, the Ukrainian SRs adopted the new name *Borotbists*. Thus, as had been the case in Latvia, when the Ukrainian Red Army advanced it was essentially pushing at an open door. The Bolsheviks talked persuasively of establishing a peasants' and workers' government; it begged people to govern themselves by organizing soviets; and it summoned the peasants to seize the landed estates immediately and redistribute the land among themselves. For a few weeks, at least, important sections of the Ukrainian peasantry believed Bolshevik promises and helped establish the new government. From 6-10 March 1919 the Ukrainian Congress of Soviets held the inaugural session of the Ukrainian Soviet Socialist Republic.[43]

The Bolsheviks' opponents did not share the same sense of revolutionary optimism as the Red Army advanced westward carrying the message of world revolution. The Mensheviks were quick to point out the dangers. *Vsegda Vpered* reported on 20 February 1919 that it was likely that the Bolshevik authorities would 'repeat in Ukraine the disastrous experience they practised on central Russia, that is they will create Poor Peasants' Committees, incite one part of the population against another, incite workers against peasants, dispatch requisition detachments to Ukrainian villages, and take away bread by force of bayonets and machine guns'.[44] The problem for the Bolsheviks was that the Mensheviks were quite right. In his speech to the First All-Russian Congress of Land Deputies, Poor Peasant Committees and Communes on 11 December 1918 Lenin had clearly linked the successful development of socialist agriculture to the prospects of world revolution. With the advance of world revolution into Latvia and Ukraine, with Germany and Hungary on the near horizon, the imperative of socialist agriculture once again dominated communists' thoughts. Lenin had raised the ideologically troubling question of the interests of the middle peasants, but for most Bolsheviks the prospects of world revolution meant that such concerns could be pushed to the back of their minds.

THREE

White Victory?

In April 1919 the Bolsheviks had many reasons to be optimistic. A soviet government had been established for a month in Hungary; Germany was being shaken by industrial unrest and a soviet government had been declared in Bavaria; and Red Armies were more than holding their own in Latvia and Ukraine. World revolution, the dream which had inspired Lenin's October coup, seemed to be a reality. More than that, the civil war seemed all but over. Negotiations with the SRs had brought the Red-Green phase of the war to an end, and as for the Whites, Kolchak's advance had been checked and a counter attack launched, while General Denikin remained trapped in the distant Kuban.

It was a false dawn. The heady mixture of revolutionary rhetoric and military advance persuaded most Bolsheviks that, with History working in their direction they could begin at once to construct socialist agriculture. Ignoring the clear evidence of autumn 1918 and the repeated peasant insurrections sparked off by the activities of the Poor Peasants' Committees in Russia proper, communists in Latvia and Ukraine began to construct socialist agriculture with a foolhardy disregard for the views of what Lenin had begun to term the middle peasantry. If such ideological dogmatism had been confined to the Bolsheviks trying to export revolution to a wider world all might have been well, but it was shared by almost all Bolsheviks. Disastrously, as it turned out, Bolsheviks in the recently reconquered Don region shared the view that socialist agriculture was central to the region's development. By summer 1919 peasant revolts in Latvia, Ukraine and the Don country had opened the road to Moscow for Denikin.

Constructing Socialism in Latvia and Ukraine

In their revolutionary utopianism the worst culprits were the Latvians. Latvian communists had always been more orthodoxly Marxist than their Russian cousins. They were deeply suspicious of the peasantry and its 'petty bourgeois' aspirations. They took it as axiomatic that the working class, and only the working class, was revolutionary and that individual peasant farms were the kernel of capitalism rather than socialism. In the brief spell between the Bolshevik seizure of power in November 1917 and the German occupation of Latvia under the terms of the Treaty of Brest Litovsk in spring 1918, Latvian communists had begun to implement a land policy based on a programme adopted during the revolution of 1905. This programme stressed the differences in land tenure between Latvia and the rest of Russia. In Russia the serfs had been emancipated in 1861 with land, creating a large number of peasant small holders; in most of the territory which became Latvia, serfs had been freed between 1816-19 without land, and as a result agriculture had become more polarized, with a small class of wealthy peasants emerging among a sea of rural landless poor. To the Latvian communists this meant that class struggle between rich and poor peasants was likely and that socialist agriculture could be achieved by unleashing the anger of the rural landless poor, encouraging them to seize the property of the rural rich and establish new state farms; since the rural poor had no land, they, like Marx's proletariat, would have nothing to lose but their chains and would happily enter state farms. Returning to Latvia with the Latvian Riflemen the communist leader Peteris Stuchka could write superciliously of his Russia comrades: his party had never had to adopt the slogan 'to each peasant his own plot of land'; Latvia was more industrially advanced than Russia and had already outstripped Russia in terms of economic planning and industrial organization.[1]

When the First Congress of Latvian Soviets opened on 13 January 1919 it was dominated by the communists. Since a contingent of local Left SRs had taken part in the Riga insurrection of 2-3 January, they were allowed to operate in the soviet and act as a legal opposition, even publishing their own paper. However Stuchka had no time for them and had to be dissuaded from his original intention of closing the party down; there was to be no parallel in Latvia to the negotiations then taking place in Moscow between Volskii and the Bolsheviks.[2] In Latvia there would be no dealings with local Left SRs because the communists were determined to push ahead with their own socialist policies for agriculture. Convinced that he was introducing a more advanced form of soviet power than that being introduced in Russia, Stuchka went on to establish 239 'soviet farms' of roughly equal size; those peasants who joined them would have to bring with them all livestock, including the family cow. By April 1919 the Latvian countryside was in uproar. Everywhere 'kulak' rebellions began, although even Stuchka conceded that many of these rebellions were not led by kulaks at all but by poor peasants. In an attempt to salvage something from the wreck, the government issued appeals to its supporters to drop the word 'commune' from the description of the new farms and to avoid the use of force when establishing them. These minor concessions came too late.

For Stuchka's government the most frightening thing was that the Latvian Riflemen, far from being immune to such peasant unrest, were soon participating in it. The peasant farmers who made up the backbone of the

Latvian Riflemen relaxing by the Kremlin Bell, Moscow, 1918. By the late spring of 1919, the force was bitterly divided between communists and non-communists.

Latvian Riflemen had first shown signs of disillusionment with the Bolshevik regime as early as summer 1918 with the near mutiny of the Fourth Regiment at Simbirsk. By November 1918 they simply wanted to return home to Latvia and once home, many were disinclined to fight for a government which was not prepared to give them land. A worried government report in February noted that crowds of riflemen, who had either left their units officially or simply deserted, were having a harmful effect on the local population which had initially welcomed soviet power. The units no longer had the slightest military worth, the report concluded. By April every report from the communist fractions in the riflemen regiments sung the same refrain: non-communist riflemen had turned against communism; they were protesting against grain requisitioning; they were deserting in droves; and substantial numbers had joined 'counter-revolutionary bands'. Indeed, from May onwards Green bands were being formed. Stuchka was so perplexed at the desertion of units which in January 1918 had led the fight against Kornilov on the Don that he could only talk darkly about the malign influence of syphilis and SR propaganda. On 23 May Riga fell to forces led by the 'bourgeois' nationalist leader Karlis Ulmanis, President of the Latvian Peasants' Union; his administration immediately gave the peasants the land which the communists had refused to distribute.[3] The minority communist element within the Latvian Riflemen withdrew to Russia to continue their struggle at the vanguard of the revolution.

A similar crisis soon overtook the Ukrainian Soviet Government. If the Latvian communists had had to rely on the support of some Left SRs to help liberate Riga, and had then promptly ignored them, so too was the Bolshevik entry into Ukraine made possible by cooperation with autonomous peasant forces. In January and February 1919 the Ukrainian Red Army, led by Antonov-Ovseenko, concentrated its efforts on freeing Kiev, leaving the conquest of the south to sympathetic peasant warlords or atamans. The south-west of the country was the preserve of the Borotbist (Ukrainian SR) sympathizer Nikifor Grigoriev while the south-east was the base for Nestor Makhno and his anarchists. In its origins, then, the Ukrainian Soviet Government, formally established on 6-10 March 1919, was not a creation of the Bolsheviks alone. Indeed, for a brief moment in February 1919 Grigoriev had been involved in an attempt by the Borotbists to set up a rival soviet administration to that being established by the Bolsheviks known as the Council of Revolutionary Emissaries.

Despite the fact that the soviet regime in Ukraine was essentially a joint creation of the Bolsheviks and the local SRs (Borotbists), the Ukrainian Communist Party insisted on ruling alone, a decision taken at the Third Congress of the party held in the first week of March 1919. Equally, rather than establish soviets throughout Ukraine as originally promised, the Bolsheviks established 'revolutionary committees' in their place. In theory these committees were appointed to prepare the way for the establishment of democratically elected soviets, but, appointed by the Commissariat for Internal Affairs rather than being elected, these committees showed no sign of surrendering their power as March turned to April. Where peasants established their own soviets, these were ignored or dissolved. The reason for this abuse of democracy was not hard to find. The communist-controlled revolutionary committees established 'Poor Peasants' Committees', modelled on those which had just been dissolved in Russia. Bolshevik land policy in Ukraine restored the fiction that class struggle was developing in the countryside and that, as a result, rich peasants were hoarding grain while poor peasants wanted to hand that grain over to the Bolshevik grain requisitioners in order to feed the urban proletariat. These mythical poor peasants were, or so the local communists believed, also keen to see the development of communal socialist farming.

Rather like their Latvian comrades, the Ukrainian communists argued that the concessions Lenin had written about for the middle peasantry in Russia were not relevant to them. The local communists believed that the February 1918 land redistribution in Ukraine had led to a greater degree of class differentiation than in Russia itself and that therefore the Poor Peasants' Committees would be more effective. When at the outset of the Red Army's march to Kiev the putative Ukrainian Soviet Government had issued a manifesto on 1 December 1918 , there was no mention of communal farming; but once Kiev was taken, as February turned to March, the establishment of collective farms began. It scarcely made things better when the government announced that only half the land in Ukraine would be allocated to collective farming, for the other half was to be turned into state farms to produce industrial crops such as sugar beet and grain for vodka distilling. The communists began to draw up detailed inventories of farm equipment and livestock to ensure the new state and collective farms were adequately stocked.

Turning those farms engaged in the production of industrial crops into state farms was seen as particularly important. On 16 January 1919 the new Ukrainian Soviet Government had nationalized the sugar industry and at the same time took the opportunity of taking into state control not only the 2.75 million acres of land already owned by sugar factories but also a further four million acres of associated peasant land. Further decrees of 5 and 11 February reinforced the principle of retaining as much land as possible in large state holdings; distributing land to the poor by breaking up large landholdings, the Bolshevik policy of 1917, was now anathema. As a result of these policies 1,685 state farms were established in Ukraine. Although the Bolsheviks claimed that some of the land fund established in Ukraine would be allocated to the poor, this was of little comfort to the majority of the peasants who in many cases had already seized land which the Bolsheviks now wanted to put under state or collective control. Yet the Ukrainian communists were proud of their plans. Delegates to the Third Congress of the Ukrainian Communist Party resolved that their chief aim in agriculture was 'to transfer from individual to social farming… [establishing] the common cultivation of the land as the best means of attaining socialism in agriculture'. Lenin's warnings about the middle peasants were dismissed as pessimism.[4]

Not surprisingly, Ukrainian peasants fought back. In April 1919 there were ninety-three uprisings against Bolshevik control, several of these coordinated by a Central Revolutionary Committee headed by the Ukrainian Mensheviks (Nezalezhniki) and those right-wing Ukrainian SRs who had not wanted to join the Borotbists. In May there were a further twenty-six uprisings. To quell this unrest, but only after the personal intervention of both Lenin and Stalin, the Ukrainian communists conceded on 8 April that they should resort to the Bolshevik practice of autumn 1917 and form a coalition government by granting the Borotbists (Ukrainian SRs) seats in a new joint administration. Ten days later Antonov-Ovseenko went even further and appealed directly to Lenin: land policy, he wrote, had to be changed in Ukraine and, as a signal of this, soviets had to be established in the place of the revolutionary committees. Even the Ukrainian Mensheviks and Right SRs, what he termed 'the political voice of the middle peasant', might have to be brought into the government, for the alternative was the complete collapse of the soviet system. Lenin was not persuaded. The inclusion of three Borotbists in the government would be enough of a concession, he argued, and even then the Borotbist ministers would have to be kept under close Cheka surveillance.[5]

Lenin wanted to keep concessions to peasant political parties to a minimum while at the same time changing the peasant policy of the Bolshevik Party. He

A frontline May Day demonstration, 1919. The peasants' lack of enthusiasm could not be clearer.

had first discovered the importance of the middle peasantry in November 1918 and since January 1919 he had been warning that the blows intended for the kulak frequently fell on the middle peasant. However, the rush of blood to the head caused by the perception that capitalism was visibly collapsing in the chaos of post-war Central Europe meant that Lenin's warnings were ignored. At the Eighth Bolshevik Party Congress, 18-23 March 1919, Lenin was determined to bring home to all Bolsheviks the dangers of ignoring the middle peasantry. He explained:

> The task that faced us was to neutralize the middle peasants… But owing to the inexperience of our soviet officials and to the difficulties of the problem, the blows which were intended for the kulak very frequently fell on the middle peasants. In this respect we have sinned a great deal … The line of our Party, which has not done enough to form a bloc, an alliance, an agreement with the middle peasants, can and must be corrected.[6]

He made the same point in a congress report *On work in the countryside*: 'we must transfer our attention from the aim of suppressing the bourgeoisie to the aim of arranging the life of the middle peasant'. Thus the congress resolution finally adopted entitled *On the attitude to the middle peasants* stressed how essential it was 'to display a more considerate attitude to their needs, end arbitrary action on the part of the local authorities, and make an effort towards agreement with them'.[7] However, passing resolutions was one thing, implementing them was not nearly so easy. What finally persuaded communists that Lenin was right about the middle peasants was the Don Rebellion and its consequences.

The Don Rebellion

The Bolsheviks had won back control of the Don in January and February 1919 in a way which had many parallels with the communist advance into Latvia and Ukraine. The German-sponsored regimes in the area had been unpopular, and many of the local inhabitants welcomed the return of the soviet administration. As the Red Army advanced, so Cossacks deserted Krasnov and returned to their farms, taking their arms with them. Yet despite the Red Army's initial welcome into the Cossack heartland, mistrust quickly developed as the new authorities began to reveal their agrarian policies. In particular the plans of the so-called Don Bureau caused alarm among many Cossacks.

The Don Bureau of the Bolshevik Party had begun life as an underground communist organization, leading the political struggle against Krasnov. For this reason, perhaps, it was both hardline and inflexible. Its enemy had been the well-heeled Cossacks, those who had fawned on Krasnov and his German advisers. The Don Bureau's obsession, therefore, was to accomplish a fundamental social revolution in the region which would destroy the economic power base on which such people had relied. The association of Cossacks with the suppression of peaceful demonstrations against the Tsar's regime and their involvement both in Kornilov's attempted coup and the fighting on Pulkovo Heights made the Cossacks an easy target for revolutionary anger, and this was an association which the Don Bureau liked to encourage. These Don communists were hostile to any notion of cooperation with local popular leaders. They preferred to bring down from Moscow ideologically trained communists who recognized the need to destroy Krasnov's former power base through radical social revolution; for them talk of cooperation with local Cossack leaders was 'Menshevik-SR casuistry'.

Red Army commanders on the Southern Front were not so dogmatic. The Political Section of the Southern Front's Military Revolutionary Council, with which the Don Bureau was supposed to cooperate, was much more flexible and pragmatic in its dealings with local politicians. If deals with sympathetic local leaders could mean the Red Army advancing without bloodshed, then so much the better. Social revolution, even if appropriate in the long run, could be put on hold.[8] The disagreement between the Don Bureau and the Southern

Front command over whether or not to collaborate with local Cossack leaders soon became focused on the personality of ataman Filip Mironov. Mironov had a revolutionary pedigree going back to the 1905 revolution, when he had protested at the use of Cossack troops to suppress demonstrators. In summer 1918 he had formed the first small Red Cossack partisan group which began to resist Krasnov's rule and in January 1919 he had led these forces back into the Don. To the Southern Front command Mironov was a valuable ally who needed to be kept on board; for the Don Bureau, and for Stalin, his forces were politically unreliable.[9]

As this dispute developed Moscow sided firmly with the Don Bureau. On 24 January 1919 the Bolshevik Party's Organization Bureau issued what became a notorious circular calling for the 'wholesale destruction of all the upper elements of Cossack society', or decossackization. Decossackization could mean many things. The most important single issue concerned the wholesale movement of populations. The Don Bureau endorsed a plan whereby peasants from central Russia would be settled on Cossack land in order to change the social mix of the area once and for all. The Southern Front command, terrified that decossackization would alienate the support of commanders like Mironov, sent a special emissary to stop these population movements happening. When the Eighth Party Congress opened on 18 March, the row was transferred to Moscow. The Don Bureau delegate proposed the wholesale transportation of the Cossacks 'to the depths of Russia', while other Don Bureau supporters argued that terror was the only policy the Cossacks would understand. Representatives of the Southern Front command took the opportunity of arguing with equal force that it was essential to negotiate with potential allies like Mironov.[10]

Given the Red Army's opposition to the plan for the wholesale movement of populations, and the sheer logistical nightmare involved, it was not surprising that little was achieved. However, there were other ways of ending once and for all the 'reactionary' power of the Cossacks: their land could be confiscated and terror used against any who resisted. An order of 5 February established three-member revolutionary tribunals to cope with any Cossacks who resisted the confiscations, thinly disguised as an agrarian reform. On 18 February a further decree allowed for the confiscation of carts, horses and fodder. On 1 March the party sent round a circular letter to party members which sought to codify the necessary measures. It began by reminding them that the lesson of the civil war so far was that 'Cossack high-ups' were the enemy and had to be brought to justice, a process which meant no compromises and no concessions. After such a hardline preamble, the first point followed logically: the rich Cossacks were to be subjected to mass terror; as to the middle Cossacks, all measures were to be taken to guarantee that they organized no demonstrations against soviet power. The second point called for the confiscation of all grain and all agricultural products, and, after other points dealing with the settling of poor farmers on Cossack land, the circular letter ended by calling for all Cossacks to be disarmed by a specified date or risk execution on the spot. A decree of 10 March ordering the confiscation of saddles sought to deprive Cossacks not only of their weapons but also their horses.[11]

Just how many Cossacks died in this decossackization campaign has been hotly debated by both survivors and historians. In what was perhaps the worst single incident the Cossacks themselves recorded 260 deaths in one village, Kazanskaya. After the event the Don Bureau was keen to argue that decossackization had never really got off the ground and that the number of deaths was limited; nevertheless the Don Bureau conceded 600 deaths in the Veshenskaya area. These figures relate to the time before the rebellion began. Once the rebellion had begun, and the Red Army was engaged in trying to suppress it, the number of executions rose dramatically to at least 8,000. In its attempt to suppress the rebellion the Don Bureau resisted all calls for moderation and, even after criticism from Moscow, stuck to its policy of brutal repression. That policy had listed the following suitable responses to Cossack resistance: the burning of homesteads; the shooting of one in five or ten of the male population in affected villages; and the mass detention of hostages in neighbouring areas. What the Don Bureau represented to its critics as a policy aimed at the 'quick and decisive neutralization of counter-revolutionaries' ended up with sixty-five mutilated bodies being found in the building used by one of its revolutionary committees.[12]

These executions took place because Cossacks resisted the confiscation of their land. The land was, of course, being confiscated for a purpose. Yet despite the stated objective of using expropriated land to help the poor, much of the land confiscated from so-called rich Cossacks did not find itself divided among the needy but was incorporated into new state farms. Even loyal communists realized that this was the crux of the matter. Communists in the regional centre of Mikhailovka, near Ust Medveditskaya, recorded an account of a public meeting held about 9 March to discuss current policy. All had gone well until the question of 'communally tilling the soil' was raised. 'No communes here, be off with you' cried the crowd who saw communists as 'robbers'. Depriving Cossacks of land in order to construct communes was only one aspect of this policy. The Bolsheviks had also banned free trade as a symbol of capitalist exploitation, while at the same time withdrawing the old Kerensky currency. As Mironov told the same meeting:

> Markets cease to operate, commercial enterprises are closed down, social life dies away, while we enter on a period of wild lawless excess. Food is taken away, they slap on every form of taxes, even demanding contributions from the men serving in the Red Army, until one is forced to complain 'well just look at the commune, God save us from a commune like that'.[13]

Just as in Latvia, the communists on the Don were following more grandiose policies than those advocated by Lenin, and in the process were fostering rebellion.

The presence of Mironov at the Mikhailovka meeting which had turned so difficult for the local communists only highlighted the dilemma of whether or not to cooperate with popular local leaders. Men like Mironov were not only prepared to criticize experiments in communal farming but also got to the heart of the undemocratic way in which the local communists chose to rule. Mironov argued that the way to establish soviet power in the region, far from the use of terror, was to abandon the establishment of revolutionary committees, which operated on the Don just as they did in Ukraine. In their place Mironov wanted to organize a series of congresses to elect new popular soviets, ending the system of naming appointees from the centre. For good measure, although he thought it followed logically from the election of free soviets, he called for an end to grain requisitioning and the introduction of 'firm' grain prices. As decossackization gathered pace Mironov's views became increasingly embarrassing to the local communists. On 24 March he was transferred out of the region.[14]

Mironov's transfer had been prompted by the start of the Don rebellion a fortnight earlier. It was at first a simple enough affair. A Cossack, tipped off that he was about to be arrested for opposing the agrarian reform, decided to resist arrest. He gathered 500 sympathizers and on 10 March seized the village of Kazanskaya; the rebellion quickly spread to the bigger settlement of Veshenskaya, and then to the rest of the Upper Don. The aims of the rebellion were made clear in a proclamation issued on 14 March and were echoed in every subsequent peasant insurrection against Bolshevik power: 'The rebellion is not against the power of the soviets and Soviet Russia but only against the party of communists who have taken power into their own hands in our native land,' it began, and ended with the slogans 'Down with the commune and shootings! Long live people's power!' This hostility towards attempts to establish 'communes' led many Cossacks to argue that they were for the Bolsheviks, who had passed the Land Reform of February 1918, but against the Communists, who were trying to take that land away. Similar views would be heard in later peasant insurrections, and reflected the simple fact that at the time of the break with the Left SRs, Bolshevik agrarian policy had fundamentally changed.[15]

However, if the Cossacks had begun their rebellion by defending the soviets, as the struggle continued they decided to make overtures to Denikin. By the end of March P.N. Kudinov had emerged as the movement's leader, and his organization claimed to control 10,000 square kilometres centred on Veshenskaya. At first, throughout April, the rebels fought by themselves having no contact with Denikin. However by May contact of a sort had been established. On 9 May Denikin used one of his British airplanes to land an emissary to Kudinov's rebel forces. By 15 May regular air drops of arms and

Plate 1 – *Exploited peasants are liberated by the Red Army, but victory is short-lived because of desertion and the return of the old order (Vasilii Spasskii, 1919). See p.159*

Plate 2 – Kolchak's ambitions and brutality: land and factories for the capitaists; gallows for the peasants (Victor Deni, 1919). See p.159

Plate 3 – 'Shoot every tenth worker and peasant' (Victor Deni). See p.159

Plate 4 – Poster denouncing Denikin (Victor Deni). See p.159

Plate 5 – Appeal for Wrangel to be crushed before reconquering the Donbas (Dmitrii Moor, 1920). See p.159

Plate 6 – Classic image of the 'kulak', with bourgeois aspirations, in contrast with the poor peasant on the brink of starvation (Vladimir Lebedev, 1920). See p.159

Plate 7 – 'If you do not want to end up feeding the landlords, you must feed the Red Army' (Vladimir Lebedev). See p.160

Plate 8 – Poster questioning whether the Cossack soldier is with the Red or the White Army (Dmitrii Moor, 1919). See p.160

Plate 9 – Anonymous poster implying that the SRs are traitors and 'defenders of the old gang of landowners and bourgeois. See p.160

Plate 10 – The SR dilemma: 'Ask an SR what does he believe, he'll tell you land to the peasants, but the peasants to whom? – to the English' (Vladimir Lebedev, 1920). See p.160

Plate 11 – A 1919 cartoon attacking the Mensheviks (Vladimir Mayakovskii)

ОБМАНУТЫМЪ БРАТЬЯМЪ
(ВЪ БѢЛОГВАРДЕЙСКІЕ ОКОПЫ).
Посланіе первое ДЕМЬЯНА БѢДНАГО.

Plate 12 – 'To our deceived brothers' (Alexander Apsit, 1918)

Plate 13 – 'Have you volunteered yet?' (Dmitrii Moor, 1920)

Plate 14 – 'You must work, with your rifle at your side' (Vladimir Lebedev, 1920)

Plate 15 – 'Now I too am free' (author and date unknown)

Plate 16 – May Day poster (author and date unknown)

Red Army men trying to shoot down a plane, spring 1919.

other supplies were taking place and the two forces began to coordinate their activities properly. Then on 24 May Denikin's Army crossed the river Donets and advanced towards the rebels, finally making direct contact with them on 8 June. By linking up with the Don rebels Denikin had broken out of the Kuban where he had been confined for so long and gained access to the whole of Ukraine.[16]

With their military position worsening all the time the Bolshevik response to the rebellion was confused. On 5 April the Southern Front command had agreed to distinguish clearly between active participants in the rebellion and other Cossacks; those uninvolved were to be left in peace and allowed to keep land and cattle, while mass terror was to be used against any active participants.[17] Such a dividing line was never as clear as it seemed. As the Bolsheviks tried to restore control over the region, they found many of their own troops unwilling to act according to the brutality of these orders. Frequently the fighting stopped while unofficial parleys took place, and on occasion these would end in defections to the rebels. Perhaps not surprisingly given the tradition of SR strength in Penza, in April the Red Army's Serdobsk Regiment, largely recruited from Penza, defected *en masse*. A month later

Trotsky informed Lenin that the reason why the rebellion could not be crushed was demoralization.

When it was far too late, Lenin himself realized that the Cossacks were not so different from other peasants and needed to be conciliated. Initially he had favoured those taking a tough line: he made no protest when Mironov was transferred from the region and when in late April Moscow debated the actions of the Don Bureau Lenin questioned whether those seeking to avoid the use of force were right, suggesting that new troops could be sent to the area if it was necessary to administer 'savage and implacable retribution'. Only on 3 June, when Denikin had already successfully taken advantage of the rebellion, did Lenin protest against harmful extremism. He wrote:

> In its order No. 27 the Revolutionary Committee of the Don Oblast has abolished the term *stanitsa*, replacing it by the designation *volost*, in accordance with which it is dividing Kotelnikov district into *volosts*. In various districts of the *oblast* the local authorities are forbidding men to wear traditional Cossack trouser stripes [*lampasy*] and are abolishing the word 'Cossack'. In the Ninth Army horse harness and carts are being requisitioned wholesale by Comrade Rogachev. In many places in the *oblast* the usual local fairs are forbidden. Austrian PoWs are being used as commissars in the *stanitsas*. We must point out how essential it is to be particularly careful about interference in such like details of daily life, which has absolutely no effect on politics in the wider sense and at the same time greatly annoys the local population.

However, it was not until August 1919 that such views were stated in public and an appeal printed at Lenin's instigation which talked of the worker-peasant government supporting freedom for all. It added:

> [The Soviet Government] has no intention of decossackifying anyone by force, it is not against the Cossack way of life, but leaves the honest working Cossacks their *stanitsas* and villages, their lands, the right to wear whatever uniform they like. It preserves their crafts and trades, permits local enterprises, which may employ paid workers up to ten in number, and gives assistance to these enterprises, allowing them to trade their products at fairs, markets and shops.[18]

The Atamans Rebel

As the Don rebellion had shown, when the Bolsheviks pursued their ideologically inspired anti-peasant policy, usually but not exclusively in the exuberance of imminent world revolution, Red-Green tensions could emerge during the struggle with the Whites. This would be repeated on a similarly dramatic scale in Ukraine. On 7 May Ataman Grigoriev staged a rebellion. He was the most important of the commanders who supported Antonov-Ovseenko's Red Army forces in spring 1919 and he had been largely responsible for harrying the French forces which had briefly landed in Odessa and occupied some of the Black Sea coast from 18 December 1918 to 6 April 1919. Grigoriev's defection meant the Bolsheviks lost most of the south-west. His motivation was the same as that of the Don rebels. He wanted an end to Bolshevik agrarian policy and the replacement of revolutionary committees with democratic soviets. He acted in the name of the Borotbists (Ukrainian SRs), although right up until the last moment the Borotbist leaders, who were about to be invited to join a coalition government with the Ukrainian Bolsheviks, pleaded with him not to rebel. Ultimately Grigoriev did not accept that the policy of forced collectivization would be abandoned simply because one or two individual Borotbists were invited to become government ministers. In Grigoriev's last message to Antonov-Ovseenko he stated: 'only the free participation of all soviet parties will give us a government… The people will be delivered from the Cheka and the dictatorship of the communists'.[19]

Although Grigoriev's rebellion was short-lived and soon repressed, it marked a significant stage in the disintegration of the Soviet Ukraine. It was not an isolated rising touched off by the whim of an irresponsible adventurer, as Grigoriev's many opponents have portrayed it, but a manifestation of the elemental political and social aspirations of millions of peasants; it sparked a series of smaller risings in its wake.[20] A report on Grigoriev, drafted by Antonov-Ovseenko himself and sent to Moscow ironically on the very day the rebellion began, made clear that what prompted the rebellion was the 'tactless behaviour of some agents of the Cheka' and the policy of forced food requisitioning. Grigoriev had great popularity among the peasantry. He always defended their interests, was modest in his own life style, and imposed strict discipline. Contrary to the common assertion that Grigoriev deliberately provoked anti-semitic pogroms, Antonov-Ovseenko believed he had succeeded in averting pogroms in Nikolaev, Odessa and Aleksandriya. His only failing was a headstrong character, which Bolshevik emissaries had still not managed to tame.[21]

In the aftermath of the Grigoriev rebellion the Bolsheviks did what they could to retrieve the situation. Ukrainian Mensheviks (Nezalezhniki) were allowed back into the soviets and the Borotbists were finally brought into the government. Although the Poor Peasants' Committees were not abolished, they were radically changed; by the end of May middle peasants had been told they would be allowed to join the Poor Peasants' Committees, thus broadening participation significantly. In a self-critical report the Ukrainian communists conceded that, rather than seeking the support of the middle peasant, the party had spent three-quarters of its time hunting for kulaks.[22]

The Bolsheviks' greatest fear was that Grigoriev might strike an alliance with the other ataman who had helped free Ukraine, the anarchist leader Nestor Makhno. Makhno, active in the 1905 revolution and President of the Gulyai Polye Soviet in 1917, began his military career by engaging in guerrilla resistance to the German occupiers in the summer of 1918. As the Germans left, he took control of a large area based around Gulyai Polye and established an anarchist administration there which lasted from November 1918 to June 1919. Unlike in Bolshevik areas of Ukraine, where talk of restoring soviets remained just talk and in their place revolutionary committees were established to prepare the ground for Poor Peasant Committees, in Makhno's domain democratically elected soviets existed. The First Regional Congress of Peasants', Workers' and Insurgents' Soviets was held on 23 January 1919. This, according to anarchist tradition, was a spontaneous meeting organized by no-one. A Second Regional Congress was held on 12 February and was quite different in character. It established a Regional Revolutionary Military Council, charged with forming an army of volunteers to defeat Denikin. This regional command then ran Makhnovite territory for the next five months.[23]

At first the Bolsheviks looked for cooperation with Makhno. After they had secured Kiev, they turned their attention to the Tauride and Ekaterinoslav Provinces and contacted Makhno to invite him to bring his forces under the wing of the Red Army. Makhno agreed under the following terms: a) his Insurgent Army would retain its internal organization intact; b) it would receive political commissars appointed by the communist authorities; c) it would only be subordinated to the Red Supreme Command in strictly military matters; d) it could not be removed from the front against Denikin; e) it would receive munitions and supplies equal to those of the Red Army; and f) it would retain its name of the Revolutionary Insurgent Army and its anarchist black flag. Despite this agreement, relations between the local Bolsheviks and Makhno were not good. The Ukrainian Bolshevik press constantly argued that the anarchists' failure to establish Poor Peasants' Committees meant that the Makhnovites were a 'kulak' organization, representing only the rich peasants. Feeling the Bolsheviks gradually encroaching on the authority of their regional command, the anarchists convened their Third Regional Congress on 10 April 1919. This worsened relations still further since during it the commander of Bolshevik forces in the area declared the assembly and its organizers 'counter-revolutionary'.[24]

Antonov-Ovseenko, on the other hand, was keen to keep contacts with Makhno open, just as he had favoured working with Grigoriev. A report in the Ukrainian Soviet Government's official newspaper, the *Kharkov Izvestiya,* for 25 April entitled 'Down with the Makhnovshchina!' infuriated him and he decided to visit Makhno in person. His own report to the Ukrainian Soviet Government of 29 April stressed the very opposite and concluded that Makhno was an asset and should not be hounded. He stressed that Makhno allowed the communist party to circulate its party literature freely, that

Makhno accepted the political commissars the Bolshevik Party had sent to him, and that he played no part in what was described as 'anti-soviet agitation'. In particular Makhno had not attended the controversial Third Regional Congress nor signed any of its resolutions. Antonov noted also that even the traditional anarchist principle of electing officers, which the Red Army had banned early in 1918, was gradually dying out. He concluded that Makhno would not move against the Bolsheviks and that if more political work were done in the area cooperation between the two forces was quite possible; the press campaign against Makhno should therefore cease and a joint struggle begun against Denikin.[25]

To try and smooth over relations with Makhno the Bolsheviks sent in the man always used in Red-Green negotiations, the man who had led the Bolshevik delegation to the Railway Union talks in November 1917 and negotiated the deal with the SRs in February 1919, Lev Kamenev. He arrived in Kharkov, the seat of the Ukrainian Soviet Government, on 19 April and a fortnight later, on 4-5 May, acting in the capacity of Extraordinary Plenipotentiary of the National Defence Council, visited Makhno. His task was to persuade Makhno to dissolve his regional command, since it weakened the common front against Denikin. In this precise mission he failed, but the talks went well in other ways. As an anarchist witness to the events recalled, 'Kamenev embraced Makhno and assured the Makhnovists that the Bolsheviks would always find a common language with them as with all true revolutionaries, and that they could and should work together'. Kamenev was *en route* for a similar mission to Grigoriev when Grigoriev rebelled. Kamenev therefore appealed to Makhno, on 12 May, to take up arms against Grigoriev. Makhno refused, insisting that he needed to seek clarification first as to why Grigoriev had rebelled. As Grigoriev's forces seized control of Aleksandriya, Elizavetgrad (Kirovograd) and Znamenka and approached Ekaterinoslav (Dnepropetrovsk), Makhno sent a delegation to Grigoriev, which proposed that Grigoriev's forces should join those of Makhno in a common Green struggle. Agreement was not reached and Makhno concluded that Grigoriev was an adventurer who had exploited genuine peasant anger to his own ends. This appears to have meant simply that Grigoriev refused to accept Makhno's merger terms.[26]

Redeploying their already stretched resources, the Red Army succeeded in confining Grigoriev's forces to the south west. Then at the end of May, when the Grigoriev danger seemed over, the Bolsheviks resolved to avoid the risk of any more such adventures by ending Makhno's independence. For some time the Bolsheviks had been starving the anarchists and their regional command of weapons and other supplies, and Makhno's forces had begun to retreat before Denikin's advance as early as 19 May. Now the whole Gulyai Polye area was blockaded and Trotsky arrived full of venom against the Makhnovshchina calling it on one occasion 'anarchist kulak debauchery'. The moment to strike came on 30 May when the regional command resolved to call an Extraordinary Congress of Soviets for 15 June to debate the growing danger from Denikin. This congress the Bolsheviks denounced as a deliberate attempt to fan the flames of a new Grigoriev revolt, and so they launched an all-out military attack on the anarchists. Under pressure from both fronts, since he had been retreating before Denikin's superior forces for the past ten days, Makhno had no choice but to surrender his capital Gulyai Polye to Denikin on 6 June. Despite the recent fighting between the Red Army and the Insurgent Army, and the arrest of many of Makhno's officers, the local Bolshevik commander Kliment Voroshilov sent Makhno an armoured train to help him escape Denikin's advance.[27]

As the Red Army prepared to retreat northwards, Makhno instructed the majority of his forces to operate within the Red Army. Then he gathered around himself a small band of his most loyal supporters to resist Denikin's westward advance in Ukraine. For several days he delayed Denikin's advance by holding the bridge over the Dnieper at Aleksandrovsk (Zaporozhe), but he was then forced to retreat further west to Elizavetgrad (Kirovograd) and so to the north of Kherson Province where what remained of Grigoriev's forces had been confined. At a mass meeting of some 20,000 irregulars near Aleksandriya, held on 27 July with the specific purpose of merging the two partisan forces, Grigoriev allegedly proposed collaboration with Denikin in the struggle against the Bolsheviks. He was gunned down on the spot by Makhno and his closest associates. Whatever his disagreements with the Bolsheviks, Makhno remained a revolutionary and had no time for Denikin. The Insurgent Army might be fleeing westwards and the Red Army northwards, but they still had the anti-Denikin cause in common. Makhno's retreat continued until 25 September, by which time his forces had established a resistance line at Uman, due south of Kiev.[28]

Denikin's Advance and the Crisis in Moscow

For three months in spring 1919 the Bolsheviks expended as much energy coping with the actions of the Don rebels and mutinous atamans as they did fighting the Whites, a point symbolized by one of Lenin's telegrams sent towards the end of April 1919 which made clear that Antonov-Ovseenko should make exporting the revolution to Hungary a second-order task, his priority being to send troops to help crush the Don rebels.[29] The result was inevitable. The combined impact of the Don Rebellion and the atamans' revolt enabled General Denikin to escape from the Kuban. The fact that the Red-Green tension of that spring was essentially a self-inflicted wound was something the Bolsheviks realized only very late in the day, despite Lenin's warnings. As the prospects for world revolution faded, so too did talk of socialist agriculture and Poor Peasants' Committees.

At the start of March 1919 Denikin's position had seemed difficult in the extreme. He faced odds of three to one on all sides of his redoubt, but the Reds'

A Red Army unit approaching the front, summer 1918.

growing internal difficulties meant they were unable to deliver a knock-out blow. Their main offensive in March was supposed to come in the Donbas, where the Thirteenth Red Army faced one of Denikin's most experienced officers, General Z. Mai Maevskii. Making the best of a secure railway supply route and skilled cavalry, Mai Maevskii held the Red Army at bay throughout April. The Red Army, meanwhile, was constantly required to divert attention to put down the Don Rebellion and could never capitalize on its position. At the other end of the Kuban the Red Army had more success. The Tenth Red Army attacked from Tsaritsyn south-west along the railway line to Krasnodar. Unusually for the Red Army, the advance was spearheaded by cavalry, and for a while the Red cavalry seemed unstoppable, advancing to only fifty miles short of Rostov. Although Denikin at first took personal charge of rebutting this threat, he handed over control to General Wrangel. At a crucial battle in the middle of May fought where the Novorossiisk-Tsaritsyn Railway crossed the River Manych, Wrangel succeeded in outflanking the Tenth Red Army, driving back its remnants in disorder, and capturing 55 canon, 100 machine guns and 15,000 prisoners. Although still two hundred miles from Tsaritsyn, Wrangel informed Denikin that the city would fall within three weeks. It was not quite that simple. His first cavalry assault of mid-June failed, but reinforcements soon arrived, including some newly delivered British tanks which were able to penetrate the barbed wire defences of the city; Tsaritsyn was successfully captured on 30 June. At Tsaritsyn Denikin captured two armoured trains, 131 railway engines, 10,000 trucks, 70 canon and 300 machine guns.

The loss of Tsaritsyn alone could have spelled disaster for the Bolsheviks, but it coincided with the chaos in southern Ukraine brought about by the Don rebellion and the revolt of the atamans. Even if Makhno's forces had not found themselves attacked by the Red Army in the north at the same time as Denikin attacked from the east, they would have found it difficult to resist the White advance. Makhno's lightly armed irregulars were no match for the new tanks which, as at Tsaritsyn, were deployed to devastating effect. In parallel with Wrangel's advance to Tsaritsyn, the White Army seized the initiative and rolled back the Thirteenth Red Army, which retreated for some two hundred miles. Belgorod fell on 23 June, Kharkov on 25 June and Ekaterinoslav on 30 June, before the front was stabilized and a line held which the Red Army would be able to defend until early September.[30]

The disastrous situation on the Southern Front provoked a major crisis in the Bolshevik camp, culminating in the dismissal of the Red Army's Commander-in-Chief Vacietis on 4 July 1919. The row had been brewing for some time. Vacietis's problem was simple: he had to decide whether Kolchak or Denikin posed the greater threat to the regime he was instructed to defend. On 18 April, in a long report to Lenin, he bemoaned how difficult it was to build up the necessary resources to cope with the reconquest of Perm when potential reserve units were constantly being redeployed to face Denikin. At this stage Denikin was perceived as an irritant. Three weeks later the situation had changed. On 7 May Vacietis informed Lenin that Kolchak had been checked and that his increasing concern was the situation on the Don, where, he conceded, the enemy had superior forces despite every effort made so far to send spare troops to the south.[31] Vacietis, then, clearly saw that there were objective reasons for the Red Army's plight, specifically that the Red Army's best troops had been sent to fight Kolchak on the assumption that Denikin would never become more than the irritant he had been in April. Others preferred to explain the Bolsheviks' problems with reference to subjective rather than objective factors, in short, with betrayal.

On 17 May Stalin was ordered to Petrograd to help shore up the defences of the city against attack from the forces of General N.N. Yudenich. Yudenich, who had been involved in counter-revolutionary conspiracies since the moment the Bolsheviks seized power, had found a base for himself in Estonia which, with the collapse of the neighbouring Latvian Soviet Republic, and with British support, had become firmly established as an independent nation. Now the Baltic, like the Black Sea, was open to Allied shipping, and Yudenich, like Denikin, could benefit from British supplies. Early in May his advance began and his progress was rapid. Stalin arrived to defend the cradle of the revolution on 19 May and by early June was convinced that the root cause of the poor state of preparations was high-level treason. He insisted on 4 June that the local Red Army commander be transferred from the front, and argued that there was a counter-revolutionary conspiracy in the city: Yudenich's advance would be coordinated with 'organized treason' in Petrograd itself and some sort of landing from the British fleet of twenty-three ships which patrolled the Baltic.

A mass grave, witness of atrocities carried out by Yudenich near Narva.

Stalin found the core of the conspiracy among the battery commanders of the naval forts in the Kronstadt fortified area which guarded naval access to Petrograd's port.[32] While Stalin may have exaggerated the extent and danger of the counter-revolutionary conspiracy in Petrograd, it was nonetheless very real. Since the start of the year the British secret agent Paul Dukes had been active both in funding underground anti-Bolshevik organizations and in penetrating the inner councils of the ruling party. His reports to London made clear that he attended at least two meetings of the Northern Front command at Kronstadt attended by Trotsky; on one occasion he sent London the full minutes of such a session, which outlined the depth at which mines were laid to protect the Baltic Red Fleet. Supporting Dukes were British sailors based in Finland equipped with fast, low-draught motor launches. These were used when, to facilitate Yudenich's march on Petrograd, the naval forts at Krasnaya Gorka and Seraya Loshad rebelled and started bombarding Kronstadt on 13 June.[33] After four days of bombardment and counter-bombardment between the rebel fortresses, the Kronstadt base and the Red Fleet, British low-draught motor launches were sent in to fire their torpedoes and generally add to the mayhem. On 16 June Stalin informed Lenin that the worst of the threat was over. But he insisted that he and his party supporters had only succeeded because they had had the courage to stand up to the military professionals whose loyalty was suspect.[34]

Stalin returned to Moscow from Petrograd fearful that the plot he had discovered might extend to the Red Army's General Staff, and this set the context for the dismissal of Vacietis. Vacietis was a blunt military commander, who took little interest in the niceties of politics. In a report to Lenin dated 18 April 1919 he had explained how short he was of experienced staff and how difficult it was when his few experienced officers were plagued by the attention of Bolshevik military commissars, few of whom had 'sufficient education to understand the feelings and the milieu over which they have to exercise control'. 'Every commissar,' he went on, ' has his secret desire to catch our staff officers out in some counter-revolutionary attitude or treachery.' Vacietis denounced this as 'a typical feature of the gendarmes of the old regime' and went on to complain about the sudden arrest of the Military Director of the General Staff's Operations Section.[35] Arrests like this, and arbitrary executions of commanders, damaged the reputation of soviet power, he warned. Such criticisms cannot have been welcomed by the Bolsheviks' security services and no doubt fuelled suspicions about Vacietis's conduct. Vacietis was arrested and detained for nine days, during which time the Central Committee issued a circular letter warning of the danger of treachery among military specialists.[36]

However, despite the fact that in the aftermath of this crisis the party's control of the General Staff was strengthened, there was never any serious suggestion that Vacietis was a counter-revolutionary. What led to his dismissal was essentially a debate about strategy which had already been reflected in the

Red Army Commander-in-Chief Vacietis touring the front.

telegrams of April and May 1919. Relations between Vacietis and the commander of the Eastern Front, Sergei Kamenev, were not good. When Kamenev had asked for additional reserves early in April, Vacietis had complied but had done so unwillingly and questioned why they were needed. Kamenev had wanted the troops to start a manoeuvre which would first outflank Kolchak and then send him to flight. For Vacietis such a policy was unrealistic given the worsening situation in the south. He was convinced that the time had come for the Red Army to cease its pursuit of Kolchak; instead, reserves should be built up and moves taken to finish Kolchak off in spring 1920, there being too many pressures on the southern front to allow for Kolchak's complete defeat. Kamenev argued that Vacietis had grossly over-estimated Kolchak's reserves and that such restraint was unnecessary. In May

Trotsky (left) talking to the Red Army's first Commander-in-Chief and former leader of the Latvian Riflemen I.I. Vacietis and other officers. Trotsky and Vacietis agreed closely on strategy and were allies during the 1919 crisis.

Vacietis persuaded Trotsky to remove Kamenev from the command of the Eastern Front, but after an appeal to Lenin, Kamenev was reinstated. Not surprisingly the animosity between the two men continued. Tension spilled over again on 10 June when Vacietis informed Kamenev that he had forty-eight hours to move brigades to Petrograd and Tsaritsyn to help support military operations on those fronts, stressing the move to Tsaritsyn as the most urgent. On 13 June Kamenev refused to comply on the grounds that he had no available reserves.[37]

On 15 June the Bolshevik Central Committee was brought in to decide the Red Army's strategic priorities. It backed Kamenev and the policy of pursuing Kolchak. Given the situation on the Southern Front this decision astounded Vacietis, as it has astounded historians since. Yet there were logical reasons for it. At this time Kolchak had succeeded in staging a modest comeback. Although further south his forces were retreating, in early June General Gajda, it will be recalled, had taken Glazov; he held it for ten days, meaning his forces were two-thirds of the way to Vyatka and the removal of the last serious obstacle to the long anticipated rendezvous with Allied forces descending from Archangel via Kotlas. There was also the diplomatic danger, certainly present in Lenin's mind, that the Diplomatic Conference, instead of cutting off all aid to Kolchak, might decide to recognize his regime and give increased support to it.

Despite his deep reservations Vacietis abided by the Central Committee decision and ordered troops to move towards Glazov. Then, on 22 June, in an apparent change of plan, he ordered Kamenev to concentrate his attack further south via Zlatoust. These confusing orders suggested a lack of commitment to the pursuit of Kolchak and, after the fall of Tsaritsyn on 30 June, Vacietis insisted that everything should be done to stop Denikin. As far as the Eastern Front was concerned, that meant ignoring Glazov and the Trans-Siberian Railway and strengthening the flank further south so that forces could be quickly redirected against Denikin. When the Central Committee met on 3-4 July it decided to sack Vacietis for having deliberately fudged its directives and appointed Kamenev to replace him. This did not end the tension, for neither the fall of Tsaritsyn nor the capture of Ekaterinoslav could be ignored. The dispute about strategy quickly changed focus to one concerning priorities on the Southern Front against Denikin. Kamenev proposed attacking along the Southern Front's left flank, i.e. moving down the lower Volga and across the Kuban. Vacietis insisted that a direct attack across the Donbas was the better option and Trotsky, despite Vacietis's arrest, sided with Vacietis; when Kamenev's left flank policy was adopted by the Central Committee, Trotsky submitted his resignation. His request to resign was rejected by the Central Committee, but he was allowed to leave headquarters to lead the struggle on the southern front, where, as he and Vacietis had always argued, the real danger actually lay.[38]

Red Counter-attack, Red Collapse

The new Commander-in-Chief's plan was drafted on 23 July and put into operation three weeks later. The initial advance began on 14 August when General V.I. Selivachev moved to split the White forces. He advanced 95 miles and took Kupiansk on 25 August. From there he seemed on the point of successfully dividing the White forces, when he was encircled and forced to retreat, arriving back where his advance had begun on 15 September. Selivachev died on 17 September, officially of typhus but, since he had been under arrest in April 1919 when Vacietis had wanted to appoint him Commander of the Eastern Front, it is likely that rumours of his execution were accurate. The other thrust of Kamenev's plan was more successful. On 15 August the Ninth and Tenth Red Armies attacked Wrangel on the Volga. Wrangel had advanced 140 miles from Tsaritsyn since the end of June, and his forces were over-extended; his White Army soon found itself in full retreat. By 5 September Red forces were approaching Tsaritsyn and hoping to gain control of it once again.[39]

Wrangel's forces dug in and prevented the Reds taking the city. Whereas in the past it had been British tanks which were so crucial to White success, this time it was not just the tanks but British aeroplanes as well – British planes flown by RAF pilots. From the White aerodrome at Beketofka, near Tsaritsyn, B Flight, one of the three RAF flights assigned to Denikin, set off to try and stop the Bolshevik advance on Tsaritsyn, led by Budyenny's Red cavalry. They had been told to expect Budyenny's forces fifteen miles short of Tsaritsyn, and that is where they found them. To their horror, the RAF pilots realized that Budyenny had deployed his forces extremely skilfully. He had positioned a decoy force in open ground, with far larger forces hidden in a semi circle behind low hills. His plan was clearly to tempt the White forces into a trap and then encircle them. The pilots decided to launch a sustained air attack from their Sopwith Camels, diving down and strafing the ground with their machine guns. 'We formed an endless chain of attack: dive, shoot, zoom, cartwheel; the Red Cavalry was helpless', one of the participants later recalled. Wrangel was so delighted with the day's work that he went to thank all the pilots in person.[40]

Thus, by early September 1919 the Red Army's counter-offensive was in trouble. Clearly the quality of the equipment supplied by the British to the White forces had played a part, but as in the spring so too in September the Red Army found itself distracted by tension with 'Green' forces. When Denikin's advance began to gain rapid momentum in June, the Bolsheviks decided that the popular Cossack leader Mironov could be recalled from his exile on the Polish border; on 17 June he was permitted to form a special Don Cavalry Corps. His old enemies on the Don Bureau at once protested to the Central Committee arguing that Mironov was still calling for free elections to the soviets and therefore likely to be no more loyal to the Bolsheviks than Grigoriev or Makhno. Mironov's views certainly had not changed: on 24 June he sent a telegram to Lenin outlining the current political situation in the country and demanding radical change amounting to the end of the Bolsheviks' proletarian dictatorship.

> It has not been only on the Don that mass rebellion has been provoked by the doings of certain revolutionary committees, special sections, tribunals and some commissars. In reality this rebellion threatens to spread in a massive wave in peasant villages throughout the whole republic.

Insisting that he had not given his life to the revolution 'to be able to watch calmly while General Denikin rides the horse of the "commune" to stamp down the red banner of labour' he called on Lenin to summon a 'popular representative body, but not a one-party one' as the only way to motivate the population in the struggle against counter-revolution and for, using the old SR slogan, 'land and freedom'. When Mironov met Lenin on 8 July he revived his call for firm prices rather than grain confiscation, and again called for power to be vested in elected soviets rather than centrally appointed revolutionary committees.[41]

Lenin was not too taken aback by such criticism. After this meeting he is reported to have said 'we need people like this; we must make use of them sensibly'. This view was not shared by the Don Bureau. Having arrived at Saransk, where the Don Cavalry Corps was to be formed, Mironov discovered to his horror that the political workers assigned to him were those very people with whom he had clashed in February. They gave him permission neither to start work recruiting his corps nor to move any closer to the front. Mironov's decision at this time to join the left-wing SR Maximalists can hardly have improved the situation as far as the Don Bureau was concerned. In a letter to Lenin of 31 July he reminded the Bolshevik leader of Tolstoy's words that 'the Russian people have no need of proletarianization' and informed him that most peasants were rebelling against soviet rule because of the horrors perpetrated by the Bolsheviks when acting 'for the good of the social revolution'. Although he was commander of the Red Army's Don Cavalry Corps, on 1 August he issued a leaflet with the slogan:

> Down with the autocracy of the commissars and the bureaucracy of the communists and long live the soviets of workers, peasants and Cossack deputies, elected on the basis of free socialist agitation.

In mid-August he was involved in a series of meetings which voted to arrest his Bolshevik commissar critics.[42]

The Don Bureau was determined to wreck the formation of Mironov's corps. As early as 6 August a report to the Southern Army Group had expressed concern at Mironov's reliability and over the subsequent week a number of moves were made to delay the formation of the corps and break it up into smaller units; three weeks into August a further report noted the worrying parallels with the cases of Muraviev, Grigoriev and Makhno. Mironov had organized a series of meetings which damned the Bolsheviks as counter-revolutionary: the Bolsheviks, he argued, were the party of the working class, while the SRs were the peasant party; a coalition government was the logical corollary of this, but the Bolsheviks refused to agree to such a coalition, so they were the true counter-revolutionaries. The report concluded that, as the weeks passed, Mironov was providing more and more opportunities for left-wing SRs to cause trouble. Given such fears, the formation of a Don Cavalry Corps seemed a risky venture, particularly since it was to be stationed at Saransk, not that far from the regional capital of Penza, or indeed from the river Volga the traditional SR stronghold. The emissaries Mironov sent to Syzran on the Volga caused the authorities great concern.[43]

Mironov was an unusual Green commander. The distinguishing feature of a Green commander was his refusal to allow his forces to be put under the command of the Red Army. Mironov, on the other hand, wanted to be part of the Red Army. In the end his patience ran out. He was determined to fight Denikin, and when it became clear the Don Bureau would frustrate this ambition he acted. On 23 August he sent the following telegram to the HQ of the Ninth Red Army:

> I request you to convey to Southern Army Group that, seeing the Revolution destroyed and the formation of my Corps openly sabotaged, I can no longer stand idly by, for I know from the letters I have received from the front that I am expected there. I am going to the front with what forces I have to pursue the bitter fight against Denikin and the bourgeoisie. The red flags of the Don Revolutionary Corps bear the inscription: 'all land to the peasants!, all factories and mills to the workers!, all power to working people, with genuine soviets of workers, peasant and Cossack deputies, elected on the basis of free socialist agitation!' 'down with the autocratic power of the commissars and the bureaucracy of the communists who are killing the revolution!' I am not alone. Along with me goes the true heart of our nation who have suffered so much for righteousness sake, and that is our guarantee that our Revolution will be saved. All so-called 'deserters' are coming to join me and will make up that fearful force which Denikin will tremble and which communists will revere. I call on all those who love righteousness and real freedom to join the ranks of the corps.

With 4,000 men, 14 machine guns, 2,000 rifles, two field guns and 1,000 cavalry, but with no orders so to do, Mironov set off to fight Denikin independently from the communists.[44]

The Red Army was quick to respond. Budyenny was given the task of capturing him and, as was the case with Makhno, Trotsky led the vitriolic press and propaganda campaign. On 12 September Trotsky urged that Mironov be shot like a dog, while the following day he published a leaflet asserting, without any evidence, that Mironov had been in touch with Denikin. Three weeks after his strange mutiny, Mironov was captured by Budyenny on 14 September and taken to Saratov. Under interrogation he denied that he was taking his Corps over to Denikin, insisting he was an SR Maximalist who believed in 'soviets without communists'; he had acted when he did because, he said, action was needed after the fall of Tambov and the evacuation of Kozlov.[45]

The White capture of Tambov was part of one of the most famous episodes of the civil war. Although the Whites were not able to launch their decisive offensive until mid-September because of the Reds' August offensive, on 8 August General K.K. Mamontov's 8,000 strong cavalry broke through the Red lines and staged a dramatic raid deep into Bolshevik territory. Within a week they had seized Tambov, moving first north west, then south west, looting Voronezh and finally crossing back into White territory on 19 September after a foray of five hundred miles lasting forty days. Fortunately for the Bolsheviks, this campaign did much to convince peasants in areas near the front that the Whites had little to offer them, since Mamantov's main aim, apart from surprise, was to gather booty for his men; burning and looting seemed to be his goal. The raid had another beneficial side effect for the Reds. Until then Trotsky had believed that there was something intrinsically unreliable about cavalry; Budyenny's cavalry seemed reliable enough, but Mironov was a cavalry commander more typical of the breed. An embittered commentator informed Trotsky in August 1919 that his failure to give due stress to the cavalry was the Red Army's Achilles Heal. This long report stressed that Krasnov's cavalry had defeated superior Red forces in 1918, that in the first half of 1919 Denikin's cavalry had done the same, but that the obvious lessons for Red Army strategy had not been drawn. The Red Army had even occupied the Don for three months where there were adequate supplies of horses, but nothing had been done, the report went on; all that had happened was that existing cavalry units had been broken up and used simply in a service capacity for infantry units. Without Mamontov's raid, this report may have remained on the shelves like others before it. However, in September 1919 Trotsky dropped his prejudice against cavalry regiments and launched the slogan 'Proletarians, to Horse!'[46]

The new policy came almost too late. In the second half of September Denikin launched his final offensive. Although the advance took place along the whole front, it was in the Kharkov area that it was most dramatic. Kursk was captured on 20 September by forces led by General Mai Maevskii. As panic spread throughout the Red Army whole units deserted. By 14 October Orel had been captured and Moscow was clearly in sight. Ten days or so after Denikin launched his drive for Orel, on 28 September, General Yudenich marched once more towards Petrograd. By the time Trotsky arrived on 17 October to organize the defences of the city, it looked certain to fall and on 21 October the former royal palaces at Pavlovsk and Tsarskoe Selo fell to Yudenich. The Whites had nearly won.

The Denikin Counter-Revolution

With the Red Army on the point of collapse, Denikin should have been able to take Moscow. He should have been able to take advantage of the disarray within the Red Army caused by three internal rebellions led by peasant leaders opposed to Bolshevik agrarian policy. The problem for Denikin was that, just like the forces of Kolchak, his men had no political programme. Unbelievably, when, over the summer and autumn of 1919, the forces of Denikin's army began to march north and mobilize large numbers of peasants for the first time from the territory they had captured, they established no system of political training; peasants were simply conscripted on the assumption that they would willingly fight. But why should peasants fight for Denikin?

Denikin's regime was as avowedly restorationist as Kolchak's. He adamantly refused to involve any socialists in the administration of his territory. His attitude to liberals was lukewarm, although he tolerated the advice of some. The reality was that the Right dominated Denikin's advisers and only one of his generals, the Chief-of-Staff I.P. Romanovskii, did not favour the restoration of the imperial regime. Lip service only was paid towards democracy by the creation of a Special Council. Set up in October 1918, its role was to coordinate the work of the various 'departments' set up to administer the territory Denikin controlled. The Special Council was unelected and its only power was to propose laws to Denikin, who could chose whether or not to implement them. The Foreign Department was headed by the former Tsarist Foreign Minister S.D. Sazonov and one of the most important men behind the scenes at Denikin's base in Ekaterinodar was the Tsar's former Prime Minister A.V. Krivoshein.

Unembarrassed by both domestic and foreign perceptions of a Tsarist restoration, Denikin reconstituted the old imperial administrative divisions in the territory he conquered. By October 1919 approximately 40 million people lived under his rule in four military governorships: Kharkov, Kiev, Odessa and North Caucasus. The military governors, who were responsible only to Denikin and not to the Department of the Interior of the Special Council, concentrated in their hands both military and civilian authority. Ignoring liberal pleas that the democratic regional and city councils be reconstituted, Denikin preferred to ape the pre-1917 arrangements by introducing a restricted franchise relating to property ownership and length of residence. As a final check against 'democratic irresponsibility', the military governors had the right to veto any decision by a regional or city council. In the absence of any democratic structures, bureaucracy proliferated. Both the President of the Special Council and the military governors solved the problems before them by establishing committees which might or might not ever report; meanwhile the members of these committees had access to influence and were not unwilling to trade in it – official protection for gambling dens was just one example of the close interaction between bureaucracy and corruption.[47]

Land and land reform was the biggest issue Denikin faced, since his advance was partly made possible by the actions of those peasants disillusioned with the way Bolsheviks had become 'communists' and tried to socialize the land. There were influential members of Denikin's entourage who urged a radical approach. The former nationalist deputy to the Fourth Imperial State Duma V.V. Shulgin, one of the men to receive the Tsar's abdication in February 1917, was in charge of Denikin's intelligence organization, 'Azbuka'. In this capacity he was well aware of the popular mood and became a passionate advocate of land reform. At the very least, he believed, the government should legalize all pre-existing land acquisitions, before moving on to develop a clear programme of land redistribution. Yet Denikin himself failed to focus on this crucial issue.

Shortly after the Don Rebellion began, Denikin announced on 5 April 1919 that he favoured land reform in principle so long as there was some system of compensation for the former landlords. The clear impression was given that land already in peasant hands could be retained so long as compensation arrangements were made. Depending on how the compensation worked, this could have been attractive to some of those peasants disenchanted with Bolshevik policies. However, having made the grand gesture, Denikin then instructed his Special Council to establish a commission which would flesh out the details. That commission, dominated by reactionaries, only reported at the end of July and, when it did, came up with a proposal which was at variance with Denikin's April message. Instead of legalizing existing acquisitions, it called for the immediate return of all land which had changed hands since the revolution; then, three years after White victory in the civil war, a process of land reallocation would begin which would favour the former landlords by allowing them to retain approximately 1,000 acres for themselves while making the peasants pay compensation at market prices for any land allocated to them. Although Denikin rejected this proposal and established a new commission, the damage was done; the new commission took a further four months to complete its work and in the end made only minor amendments. Legislation such as this was not going to woo the peasant. Nor was Denikin's day-to-day land policy much better. In practice Denikin allowed peasants to stay on the land they had taken, but since it was not theirs, he insisted they should pay rent to the state; that rent was in the form of compulsory grain deliveries. The Bolsheviks seized grain 'in the interests of the alliance between the poor peasantry and the workers'; Denikin seized grain 'in lieu of unpaid rent for land illegally seized' – the net result for the peasant was the same.[48]

Like the supporters of Kolchak, Denikin's supporters were obsessed with the notion of revenge. In Omsk there was a ready target, the SRs who had run both the Provisional Government and the Directory. For Denikin's supporters the target was more sinister. Anti-semitism had played a prominent part in the Tsar's attempts to deflect social unrest, and this tradition became little short of the focal point of the world view of Denikin's officer corps. Pogroms against the Jewish population were routine and went through three clear stages. In June and July 1919 the Volunteer Army, mostly its Cossacks members, carried out what have termed 'quiet pogroms'. These were attacks on individual houses, families and women. By August these had become 'mass pogroms' involving large scale looting and arson against whole communities. Finally, as the Whites retreated in the autumn, pogroms turned into vicious mass murders, into what was essentially revenge on the defenceless for the sufferings of retreat and defeat. A conservative estimate put the total number of pogrom victims at 100,000 dead.

Levels of bestiality varied, as did the methods of murder. Most often the Cossacks simply shot or bayonetted their victim to death, but there were instances of hanging, burning, drowning in wells and even live burials. There were also recorded instances of men buried in sand up to their necks and then killed by having horses driven at them. That this was not simply the work of primitive thugs is clear from the memoirs and correspondence left behind by the White officer corps. The language of official reports was Hitlerian in tone: one report noted 'no administrative step would help [restore the White cause]; it was necessary to make harmless the microbe that was the Jews.' Anti-semitism allowed White officers to make sense of the collapse of their Russia without asking too many searching questions about why, in reality, the old Tsarist order had collapsed. Repeated talk of the sinister power of the Jews could be used to explain almost any turn in the White's fortune and as defeat eventually loomed the language of secret reports became increasingly shrill.[49]

Mostly anti-semitism was a negative phenomenon. However, once Kiev had been taken Shulgin became Denikin's administrator there. A convinced anti-semite, Shulgin supported efforts to develop an anti-semitic, and therefore pro-regime, workers' movement. A veteran of the 1905 revolution was recruited who on 3 September 1919 founded the Organization for the Unification of All Trade Union Workers. This so-called trade union opposed both strikes and Jews, and the Army rushed to support it, providing subsidies for a newspaper, offices in requisitioned buildings and printing presses seized from the banned socialist parties (the leader of the local army Propaganda Bureau was a former member of the Tsarist anti-semitic populist organization, the Black Hundreds). Members of the trade union, unlike other workers, were permitted to exchange their soviet money for Denikin's currency. The movement was confined to Kiev, making few converts in Kharkov and the Donbas, where Menshevik influence remained strong. Even in Kiev its membership dwindled once it became clear that the Whites' days were numbered.

Apart from this flirtation with a loyalist labour movement, Denikin had no time for labour. Yet labour should have been a major concern, given that the Donbas was about to fall into his hands. In April 1919 Denikin had asked one of his few liberal advisers to draft some labour legislation. This talked of the rights of owners, the interests of the trade unions, the importance of the eight hour day, and the need to resolve industrial disputes peacefully. Detailed implementation was left to a commission, which only reported at the end of October when the tide against Denikin was already turning. On 4 November Denikin signed legislation introducing social insurance cover and trade union freedoms. However, these, like those of Kolchak, were little better in scope than the provisions introduced by the Tsar after the 1905 revolution. As before

1917 the social insurance funds would be regulated by representatives not only of the workers and employers, but also of the Ministries of Justice and the Interior. Trade unions, although legal, would, as under the Tsar, have to register with a district court and prove details of their constitution and membership. The eight-hour day law was implemented only on 12 December when Denikin's forces had already been routed; since it allowed employers to impose four hundred hours of compulsory overtime each year its provisions were essentially meaningless.

When between April and November 1919 trade unionists tried to clarify their legal position, they met with little support. On 21 July the Council of the Southern Trade Union, dominated by moderate Mensheviks, took a memorandum of complaints to General A.S. Lukomskii one of Denikin's oldest and closest advisers and an associate of Kornilov in 1917. He told them that if any of the statements in their memorandum proved to be false they would be held responsible and punished. Attempts by trade unionists in September to hold talks with General Mai-Maevskii, by then the Military Governor of Kharkhov, were simply rebutted. Some of the more liberal members of Denikin's Special Council did try to seek cooperation with the Menshevik trade unionists. In June 1919 a liberal mine owner attached to the Special Council asked the Council of Southern Trade Unions to help draft some labour legislation; they agreed on condition strikes were removed from the control of the military courts and press freedom was established. On 20 August the trade unions were allowed to elect representatives who on15 September joined an equal number of employers' representatives for further talks. However at this meeting the workers were prevented from reading out a resolution critical of Denikin and his policies and so they walked out in protest. No more such meetings were held.[50]

The reality of labour relations in Denikin's territory was simply this: with him the former Tsarist managers returned. In the steel town of Yuzovka, the former director of the New Russia Company came back to his former works and restored the labour regime which had existed before the overthrow of the Tsar, even before the reforms of 1905. This meant public flogging was widely practised; often victims were subjected to this pre-1905 form of corporal punishment in markets and town squares for everyone to see. The returning owners seemed to be not so much concerned with increasing profits as with getting revenge; on one occasion a manager had thirteen arrested workers beaten to death. When wildcat protest strikes broke out in a desperate attempt to stop such atrocities, the strikers were mobilized and sent to the front.[51]

Despite the restorationist nature of Denikin's regime, it is clear that there was some initial enthusiasm for it. When Kharkov was captured on 24 June 5,000 new volunteers joined his army over the next three days. The price of bread fell immediately to one tenth the Bolshevik level. This honeymoon period did not last long, however. When the soviet rouble was abolished many factories closed for lack of work and unemployment rose. When Kharkov city council was reconstituted, it was dominated by moderate socialists and therefore ignored by the authorities. By August apathy had set in and by October that apathy had changed to hostility towards the Whites. The antagonism was mutual. Before they evacuated Kharkov on 12 December the Whites executed 1,000 enemy prisoners.[52]

FOUR

White Defeat,
Red/Green Stalemate

As Russia's civil war moved into its final phase, during which the White counter-revolution would be defeated once and for all, the Bolsheviks were faced by an acute dilemma. The lesson of the first half of 1919 was that victory would only be theirs if they cooperated with the Green forces combating both Denikin and Kolchak; how, then, in the aftermath of victory over the Whites could the Bolsheviks ensure they were in no way politically dependent on the Greens and retained the monopoly of power which had been theirs since spring 1918. As it became clearer that this Green 'problem' would not go away, the Bolsheviks opted for a military solution; but in a military solution ultimately tempered by economic concessions. Although in the course of 1920 talk of socialist construction, and even world revolution, was again heard, in the end the Bolsheviks settled for the concession to the peasantry known as NEP (the New Economic Policy), which restored a free trade in grain at 'firm' prices.

The Narod Group

In October 1919 General Yudenich stood outside Petrograd and General Denikin approached Moscow. The counter-revolution seemed on the point of victory. In such circumstances both Reds and Greens were ready to fight side by side. This was even the case within the territory of Soviet Russia, where a section of the SR Party agreed to develop still further the links established in February between the Bolsheviks and Volskii's Ufa Delegation. As had been the case earlier in the spring, the SR Party leader Chernov had reservations as to whether this was the correct policy and by summer 1919 the SR Central Committee and what had been christened the 'Narod' (People's) Group, after the title of its newspaper, were at loggerheads. On 18-20 June 1919 the SRs were allowed to hold their Ninth Party Council in Moscow, and this gathering became the occasion for a showdown between the two wings of the party.

Although the SRs had already agreed in February to cease military operations against the Bolsheviks, it had been made clear at the time that this was a ceasefire, not a peace settlement; the time might come when the armed struggle had to be renewed. The Narod Group now argued that the time had come to end the armed struggle against the Bolsheviks once and for all and to cooperate with all elements of the Bolshevik administration in the greater struggle against White counter-revolution. The SR Central Committee, however, remained critical of the idea of cooperating with the Bolsheviks, reminding members that it was the Bolsheviks who were responsible for the failure to establish a coalition socialist administration in October 1917. Making clear that 'the Bolsheviks' pseudo-class dictatorship was inevitably turning into a party dictatorship', the SR Party decided to stick with its third way, the formation of a third force which would organize purely political struggle against the Reds in the soviet domain and armed struggle against the Whites in all other parts of the country. There should be 'no harmful illusions that the Bolshevik dictatorship might gradually grow into popular power', the party council concluded.[1]

As far as the Narod Group was concerned, this decision was utterly mistaken. The problem posed by its neat formulation was this: armed struggle against the Whites demanded the creation of a single armed force, but how would that armed force relate to the Red Army, which represented a party with which the SRs were engaged in a political struggle. What were the limits of that political struggle and to what extent should two such armed forces cooperate? For the Narod Group, the resolution of the Ninth Party Council had resulted in confusion. In a war there could only be one army, they argued: the SRs should support the Red Army and any independent Green formations operating in the rear should coordinate their activities with it.

Over the summer and autumn of 1919 a 'literary duel' developed between the Narod Group and the SR Central Committee with both sides denouncing each other in a series of articles and pamphlets. On 23 August the SR Central Committee decided it had had enough and voted to dissolve the Ufa party organization, where Volskii had his power base. The Central Committee stood firm despite growing criticism from within the ever shrinking area of territory under soviet control. Even when Denikin had advanced to Orel, and Chernov himself felt that the time had come to make a public appeal in support of the Red Army, the SR Central Committee refused to change its stance and issued no such call. On 17 October the Narod Group wrote to the Central Committee accusing it of behaving like Pontius Pilate and washing its hands of the crucial question of support for the Red Army. In response the Central Committee met on 25 October, refused once again to make any commitment to the Red Army, and expelled the Narod Group from the party. Splits then followed in a number of party organizations.[2]

In this row, the attitude towards the Red Army was all important. The Narod Group agreed with the Central Committee on all other aspects of policy. It was critical of the undemocratic soviets established by the Bolsheviks, which they wanted to replace with genuine 'popular bodies' at the soonest possible opportunity; their call for free elections and an end to grain requisitioning had resulted in the Cheka closing the *Narod* paper. However, the Narod Group could not imagine how a war could be fought without proper coordination from the top and that meant a single command. The most articulate spokesman of the Narod Group, K. Burevoi, wrote a widely circulated pamphlet in which he urged that many people hostile to soviet power still had to recognize the horrors of Kolchak's rule and accept the simple truth: 'is the only way forward to recognize the Red Army and struggle in its ranks? Yes, it is! If the Red Army is not recognized, then one's hate for the restoration can only be platonic.' Burevoi and the Narod Group refused to recognize the legitimacy of any force other than the Red Army, even to the extent of condemning those who deserted the Red Army to form independent Green detachments. For Burevoi desertion had no political significance but was characteristic of any war; he called for the 'most active struggle against desertion, explaining to the people the disastrous consequences which could arise as a result of the existence of partisan 'green armies' with their various different governments, atamans and commanders'. Even peasant disturbances were disavowed: imagining the accusation that support for the Red Army could mean support for the Red Army's suppression of peasant insurrections, Burevoi accepted that this was indeed the case; it was the causes of insurrection which needed to be addressed, he argued, not the role played by the Red Army in suppressing them. The one concession Burevoi made to his SR past was his final call for all socialists and revolutionaries 'to join the Red *People's* Army'.[3]

Makhno, Budyenny and Denikin's Defeat

If the Narod Group of SRs believed they had to cooperate with the Red Army, so the Red Army decided it could not continue its hard line against the Green atamans, given the disaster threatening on the Southern Front in October 1919. Mironov, the SR Maximalist commander from the Don, so recently arrested for his mutiny against the authority of the Red Army, was quietly released from prison and allowed to resume the struggle against Denikin. When put on trial on 5-6 October he had been accused of wanting to become a popular hero 'like Garibaldi', of propagating policies reminiscent of those of Kerensky, and of encouraging deserters to join the Greens. He had been sentenced to death. Now, however, the death sentence passed on 7 October was commuted and he was freed by an Extraordinary Tribunal on 9 October. More significantly, on 20 October Moscow recalled from the Don Bureau those commissars who had done so much to frustrate the formation of Mironov's Don Cavalry Corps in the first place. On 26 October the Politburo agreed that Mironov could resume a command on the Southern Front.[4]

Denikin's retreat actually began at the end of September, even before his advance guard approached the gates of Moscow. The tables were turned by the apotheosis of a Green ataman, the anarchist leader Makhno. On 26 September Makhno's forces simply stopped retreating, turned, and attacked their pursuers head-on. The effect was devastating. What began as a White retreat quickly

A captured British tank, renamed 'The Moscow Proletarian' and displaying a red star.

turned into a rout. Within days Makhno had taken Aleksandrovsk (Zaporozhe), and in not much more than a week the whole of southern Ukraine had changed hands; on 20 October Makhno's forces took Ekaterinoslav (Dnepropetrovsk), posing a potential threat to Denikin's main force at Orel.[5]

Meanwhile General Yudenich had failed to take Petrograd. Although the royal palace at Pavlovsk had been lost, it was at Pavlovsk that the Red Army counter-attacked on 21 October. The assault was led by an elite group of Latvian Riflemen, transferred on Lenin's instructions to the Petrograd front from Tula, where they had been assembled to help stem Denikin's advance. This disciplined unit opened the attack and at first panicked when Yudenich sent in his British tanks. However, the officers steadied their men and succeeded in holding the line. The tanks, manned by British crews, were Yudenich's secret weapon which he was holding back for the final assault on Petrograd. Once the Latvian Riflemen had shown that the tanks were not invincible, morale among the Red troops rose and by the end of October the threat to Petrograd had dissipated.[6]

Elite Latvian units also played a crucial role at Orel. Here it was Latvian veterans who spearheaded the assault on Orel, which was recaptured on 20 October; four days later Budyenny's cavalry took Voronezh. Budyenny's triumph was quite unexpected. At the start of October he had been over one hundred and fifty miles away confronting Wrangel on the Tsaritsyn front, but, fearing a repeat of the Mamontov raid, had moved north-west and was well

Grave of those executed by Denikin before the evacuation of Orel, October 1919.

placed to seize Voronezh as the Red counter-attack began. From there Budyenny led the assault on the crucial railway junction of Kastornoe on the Voronezh-Kursk railway. Here, in what was perhaps the most important battle of the civil war, Budyenny's horsemen rode out of a blizzard in a surprise attack and succeeded in capturing the junction; it took three weeks of bitter fighting thereafter for the Whites to retreat and the Red Army to emerge triumphant. Victory at Kastornoe threatened the complete encirclement of Denikin's vanguard and the White leader had no choice but to pull back. Soon it was a rout which was only stemmed at the end of the year when a new defensive line was established back on the Don; even this line did not hold out for long.[7]

Denikin's rout was accelerated by Makhno's reconquest of Ukraine. However, given the fighting which had taken place between the Red Army and the Insurgent Army earlier in the year, it was not surprising that Makhno was a little apprehensive as his forces approached the inevitable rendezvous with the Red Army. Some of his advisers, taking the same line as the SR Party Central Committee, were keen he should keep his distance from the Bolsheviks: others, following the logic articulated by the Narod Group, favoured close cooperation with the Red Army. Among Makhno's supporters it was the anarchists who took the part of the SR Central Committee and the Borotbists (Ukrainian SRs) who took the part of the Narod Group.

Makhno's relationship with other political parties has been problematic for historians. Anarchists have always been keen to stress how Makhno had no time for 'statist' parties, even radical SRs. In truth it was not that simple. When

Makhno visited Moscow in spring 1918 he had been attracted to many of the Left SR leaders and felt that, if they would only abandon their alliance with the Bolsheviks, they could play an important role in 'deepening and broadening the revolution'. In spring 1919 the communists noted a certain distance between Makhno and his anarchist advisers and the active presence of many Left SRs, who played a big part in preparing for the planned Fourth Extraordinary Congress of Soviets. When it came to important tenets of anarchist ideology, Makhno was pragmatic rather than ideological. Although personally committed to the idea of establishing voluntary communes of poor peasants, these were the exception rather than the rule in his realm and benefitted only a few. The Second Congress of Soviets in February 1919 spoke only of the expropriation and redivision of the land, not the formation of communes. The fact that for his last campaign in 1920 Makhno's secretary was the Baltic sailor Popov whose forces had been at the core of the Left SR insurrection in Moscow in July 1918 suggests Makhno saw little of principle to separate anarchists and radical SRs.[8]

In autumn 1919, as his forces pursued Denikin, Makhno had no problem cooperating with the Borotbists (Ukrainian SRs). After the occupation of Ekaterinoslav by Makhno's forces, the Borotbist underground came into the open and official talks were held between them and the anarchists. Having committed themselves to the overthrow of Denikin, many Borotbists became commanders in Makhno's forces. In liberated Ekaterinoslav Makhno carried out his campaign promise when it came to freedom of agitation for freely elected soviets; Left SR, SR and even Bolshevik papers were allowed to circulate freely. However, as the Red Army approached the Borotbists prepared to negotiate with the Bolsheviks. They had been brought into the Ukrainian Soviet Government in May 1919 and were now willing to join the Bolshevik inspired 'All-Ukrainian Revolutionary Committee'; thereafter they rejoined the Provisional Ukrainian Government in the middle of December.

Makhno would not take this step, but nor was he ready to organize an armed clash with the Bolsheviks. Criticized by some of his anarchist advisers for not merging the many partisan forces in Ukraine into a single army capable of resisting the Bolsheviks, Makhno decided to prepare for a rendezvous with the Red Army on the ground where he felt strongest. So at the end of November he retreated from Ekaterinoslav to strengthen his base at Gulyai Polye, and there waited for the meeting with the Red Army. This finally took place at the end of December on the road from Ekaterinoslav to Aleksandrovsk. The encounter was, according to witnesses, 'warm and comradely'. A general meeting was organized at which the combatants of both armies shook hands and declared that they would 'fight together against their common enemy, capitalism and counter-revolution'. What worried the Bolsheviks and delighted the anarchist witnesses of these events, was that 'some units of the Red Army even showed a desire to go over to the Makhnovist ranks'.[9]

Just how widespread Makhno's influence was, and how dangerous he could be to the Bolsheviks, can be seen from the following report on the Budyenny

Red cavalry on the Southern Front, 1919.

Cavalry Corps. A lack of cavalry had been the Achilles Heel of the Red Army, but since Trotsky had issued the slogan 'Proletarians to Horse!' in September 1919 the Red Army had put great effort into building up its cavalry and by the end of the year the number of cavalry on both sides was almost equal. However, creating a cavalry corps had its disadvantages: skilful horsemen tended to be peasants or Cossacks rather than proletarians, making them susceptible to Makhno's propaganda. Equally, what had inspired the White cavalry – plunder and charismatic leadership – could also inspire the Red Cavalry. By December 1919 some in the Red Army were worried that Budyenny's forces were acting increasingly like a private army, engaging in plunder, idolizing their leader and, most worrying of all, showing a distinct sympathy for Makhno. In a long report to the Bolshevik Central Committee dated 13 December 1919 a military commissar detailed acts of debauchery and looting by Budyenny's men, criticized their constant toasts to his glory, described the cavalry as little more than a private army and warned that what was being created was a 'new adventurism in the style of Mironov or even Makhno'. Many of his fellow commissars, this commissar concluded, had heard the cavalry men saying: 'let's kill the Whites first, and then we can start killing the communists!'[10]

Not much more than a week after Makhno's troops had welcomed the Red Army, they received an order to redeploy to guard the Polish frontier. Believing, correctly, that this was an attempt to marginalize them, the Insurgent Army refused to go. Makhno's Insurgent Army saw itself as a co-belligerent force, not one subservient to the Red Army High Command. For them the spring 1919 agreement was still in force which prevented its deployment to any front other than the Denikin front. The Red Army saw it differently. In mid-January 1920 the Insurgent Army was declared outside the law and for the next nine months every effort was made to destroy it as Makhno's men moved erratically around Ukraine from safe haven to safe haven, always escaping entrapment at the last moment. At the time of this break with the Bolsheviks, Makhno called on the Ukrainian peasants to help him establish 'a true soviet socialist order' which really would give land to the peasants and factories to the workers. These ideas would mobilize millions later in the year.[11]

The Black Sea Greens

As Denikin retreated, he was not only under attack from Makhno's Green forces in Ukraine, but from other Green forces in his rear. To his south he faced the Green troops of V.A. Filippovskii. Filippovskii was a deputy to the Constituent Assembly, a former minister in the Komuch administration, and one of those SRs who had survived the Omsk massacre of December 1919. He managed to escape from Kolchak's territory and took refuge in Georgia, which by 1919 was an independent state run by the Mensheviks under the protection of British troops. In August 1919 Filippovskii was contacted by a Green commander operating in Denikin's rear on the Black Sea Coast and asked to join in establishing the Committee for the Liberation of the Black Sea Coast (KOCh); Filippovskii was made President and the Green commander, V.N. Voronovich became its Vice President and military chief.

Voronovich was a wounded veteran of the First World War who in autumn 1917 had established a rural cooperative for similar wounded ex-soldiers on the former estate of one of the Tsarist Empire's richest landowners near Sochi. In this idyllic backwater the revolution seemed far away. The Executive of the Sochi Soviet still had a minority of Bolsheviks as late as spring 1918, and the SR Voronovich continued to play an active role in soviet affairs throughout the summer as the population prepared to resist German incursions beyond the demarcation line established by the Treaty of Brest Litovsk. Because of his military experience Voronovich led the locally recruited military force and liaised with the Red Army which at that time still had headquarters in Ekaterinodar. He was unimpressed with the Bolsheviks he met. This was the time of the Red Terror and the execution of 28 elderly Cossacks arrested at the market for alleged profiteering convinced him that continued cooperation with the Bolsheviks was impossible. The attitude of the local Bolshevik commander, Sergo Ordzhonikidze, reinforced his decision. Ordzhonikidze wanted to impose conscription on the Black Sea region, but Voronovich insisted that the local soviet would never agree. Voronovich returned to Sochi with Ordzhonikidze's threat to shoot him as a counter-revolutionary ringing in his ears.

With the end of the First World War Sochi changed hands. Briefly occupied by Georgian troops, these were replaced by forces loyal to Denikin. Denikin's arrival resulted in a dramatic turn to the right in Sochi's political life. Many members of the old imperial regime, on their annual holiday to Sochi over the summer of 1917, had simply stayed on in the town rather than risk returning to the capital as the political situation worsened. Living quietly through 1918, the arrival of Denikin revived their political ambitions. Anyone, like Voronovich, with leftist views and a member of the soviet, was now persecuted as the revolutionary bodies established in 1917 were wound up and the pre-revolutionary administrators brought back. Denikin's land policy made clear that Voronovich's cooperative no longer had secure tenure of its land, and the threat of the military governor to dissolve all cooperatives persuaded Voronovich to wind up this venture.

When in spring 1919 Denikin tried to enforce mobilization of the local peasantry, a spontaneous Green rebellion began and Voronovich rallied to the cause. The movement was remarkably well organized. Although resistance would start at grass roots level with a village assembly, from that initial meeting a hierarchy of district and regional assemblies was constructed giving more planning and direction. This first attempt at resistance was poorly armed, and although it elected a 'People's Staff', it opted to negotiate with Denikin rather than fight him; in return for changes to the mobilization order, permission was granted to organize a peasant congress. By Easter 1919, when it had become clear to the peasants that Denikin was not prepared to honour this agreement, a second round of fighting began. This time the Green forces were more ambitious. In July 1919 an attack on Gelendzhik was planned, but called off at the last minute. In August 1919 Novorossiisk was attacked. In military terms the impact was minimal, but as with most Green activity, the main aim was to act as an irritant and to put across the message that the rear would never be secure unless policies changed.[12]

By August 1919 Voronovich's forces felt strong enough to hold a peasant congress to give popular endorsement to the temporary Organizing Committee which they had established. Infiltrated by Denikin's police, the congress was raided on 14 August and most of the Organizing Committee were arrested. Those who escaped elected a new Organizing Committee, which included Voronovich, and it was this body which took the decision to contact Filippovskii. A peasant delegate congress was subsequently organized on 18 November 1919 in the small strip of neutral territory established between Denikin's domain and the Menshevik republic of Georgia. As Voronovich noted in his memoirs, the peasants had come to the conclusion that if things were bad under the Bolsheviks, they were that much worse under Denikin. Therefore the peasant congress voted overwhelmingly in favour of starting an armed insurrection against Denikin 'so as to be able, before the Bolsheviks arrive, to establish firmly on the Black Sea coast their own peasant power.. We want no 'communes' just to be our own masters.' Later Filippovskii put this into the context of SR Party policy: 'we have always seen the Black Sea Coast as an inseparable part of Russia; if we now declare its temporary independence, that is motivated by a desire to recognize neither the All-Russian dictatorship of General Denikin, nor the similar dictatorship of the Bolsheviks'.[13]

This commitment to form a Black Sea People's Republic, temporarily separate from Russia, put Filippovskii and Voronovich firmly in line with the policies of the SR Central Committee and the concept of establishing a third force. Other KOCh leaders were closer in their political views to the Narod Group. Voronovich was a Right SR; Filippovskii stood near the party centre; however five of the remaining seven members of KOCh were Left SRs, including Voronovich's Chief-of-Staff, who spent most of his time fighting at the front rather than politicking with the committee. The importance of KOCh for the SR Party can be seen from the fact that a Central Committee member was deputed to join it. Tension between Left and Right of the party would centre, as with the Narod Group, on how much cooperation was possible with the Red Army. However at the founding congress all had been agreed on one thing: the Bolsheviks needed to end their dictatorship and form a coalition socialist government like the one which operated from October 1917 to spring 1918.[14]

On 26 January 1920, when an increasingly desperate Denikin tried once more to introduce conscription in the area, a full-scale insurrection began. It was an immediate success, moving quickly from the villages and mountains to major centres of population. On the very first day of fighting 600 men and 1,000 rifles were captured. By 4 February KOCh had taken up residence in Sochi. Organizationally these Greens quickly set about constructing the trappings of authority. Diplomatic relations were established with the Menshevik Government in neighbouring Georgia, and a treasury began to issue distinctive bank notes.[15] However, political disagreement soon followed over what to do next. Voronovich had always assumed that the Kuban Cossacks would turn on Denikin, much as his own peasants had done, and therefore would quickly rally to KOCh's side, turning the Black Sea People's Republic into a 'Kubano-Black Sea Peasants' and Cossacks' Republic'. However, when the Red Army began to advance into Kuban from Tsaritsyn, the Kuban Cossacks stayed loyal to Denikin. For Filippovskii the attitude of the Kuban Cossacks was a disappointment, but he was willing to let the Red Army clear the Kuban as their contribution to what he saw as a joint struggle. Voronovich was suspicious of the Bolsheviks, sensed they would only take KOCh seriously if it controlled a major swathe of territory, and so resolved to use British influence to persuade the Kuban Cossacks to support the Greens.

Voronovich took advantage of a chance meeting with Major Keyes, the commander of the British intervention forces. Keyes was trying to negotiate a truce between the Whites and the Greens which would enable Denikin to make good his escape from the Black Sea coast and evacuate his forces to the Crimea. Voronovich rejected out of hand the idea of a ceasefire, but persuaded Keyes to help him make contact with the Kuban Cossacks. Together they sailed to Novorossiisk, from where Keyes journeyed to Ekaterinodar promising to return with Kuban Cossack interlocutors. He returned empty handed and frustrated; Denikin had intervened to ensure no contacts were made between the Greens and the Kuban Cossacks. Before returning Voronovich to Sochi, Keyes told him: 'I want you to know that I wish you all the best and am very sad that I failed to interest Denikin in making peace with the Black Sea peasantry.'[16]

Not surprisingly, Voronovich returned to a political crisis in Sochi. His sudden disappearance to Novorossiisk with Major Keyes had been interpreted by the Left SRs on KOCh as an attempt to reach an accommodation with Denikin via the Allies. Bolshevik sympathizers in particular used the affair to question the tactics of KOCh: why, when the Red Army was coping with the situation in the Kuban was it so important to use British contacts to persuade the Kuban Cossacks to change sides? Since the Ninth Red Army was already marching across the Kuban, the obvious way forward was to make common cause with it. This certainly was the view of some of the new units which flocked to join KOCh as its triumphant march up the Black Sea Coast progressed. Voronovich's Chief of Staff was very much of this view. He felt that some of the best units at his disposal were two regiments which had first been Red Army soldiers, then Denikin's PoWs, and were now fighting with the Greens; these units had no ideological objections to cooperating with the Reds once again.

These tensions came to a head at an extraordinary peasant congress held at the end of February 1920. Red Army sympathizers, based around these PoW regiments, called themselves the 'front delegation' and made great play of their commitment to fighting rather than playing the sort of high politics in which Voronovich seemed to be engaged. Most peasant resolutions taken at the congress stuck to the KOCh formula of 'defending peasant power against attacks from left and right', whereas the front delegation called for the closest cooperation with the Red army. Voronovich tried to argue that the front delegation, with no link to the locality, could not speak for the peasants; he wanted to deprive them of the right even to attend the congress, but on this he was overruled. During the congress Voronovich's position was further undermined by the unannounced arrival of the British.

With the Green Army attacking the port of Tuapse, the British made a final attempt to bring about an understanding between KOCh and Denikin. Their emissary, General Cotton, turned up in Sochi and promised that Denikin was now prepared to enter into direct talks with the Greens and that he would concede their independence and legitimate right to administer the Sochi area on condition that the assault on Tuapse was called off. Filippovskii turned the proposal down, but agreed that Cotton could address the congress. His cool reception showed how unpopular the Allies were, and persuaded Filippovskii to distance himself completely from Voronovich and the British and to seek a compromise instead with the front delegation. Filippovskii clearly felt strongly that it was important to put unity first and win unanimous support for a compromise resolution. The result was that the congress adopted a resolution calling not only for the formation of a Black Sea People's Republic but for the federation of that republic with other parts of Russia; Voronovich's insistence that union with other regions of Russia was only possible 'where popular representatives had been freely elected' was dropped as gratuitously offensive to the Bolsheviks.[17]

The capture of Tuapse on 27 February 1920 caused more divisions within the KOCh leadership. Voronovich and Filippovskii had been keen to press on towards Novorossiisk, but a Bolshevik emissary arrived requesting help for the Red Army's campaign in Kuban. As a debate on tactics began, Voronovich's opponents called a 'front congress', established their own revolutionary military council and renamed their forces the Black Sea Red Army. This move backfired. In protest many peasant units began to leave the front. To prevent further defections the new Tuapse based revolutionary military council invited KOCh to talks on 9 March. Attended by a representative of the SR Central Committee it was agreed that KOCh could retain power in Sochi, if the revolutionary military council retained power in the frontal area around Tuapse; this would enable it to coordinate activities with the Ninth Red Army. The problem came, of course, when dividing up the spoils of war. Voronovich wanted to retain sufficient arms to enable KOCh to defend a sizable area of the Black Sea Coast from Bolshevik advance; his opponents insisted that all available arms were needed at the front. Filippovskii sided for cooperation with the Bolsheviks, saying: 'what do we need all those guns and bullets for when the final defeat of the volunteers is close at hand'.[18]

The last weeks of fighting on the Black Sea Coast were chaotic. So many Green troops moved to help the Ninth Red Army that both Tuapse and Sochi were temporarily retaken by the Whites and KOCh was forced to escape to the hills. But these were the death throes of the Whites. On 30 April 1920 the Red Army arrived in Sochi and in mid-May the new Bolshevik administration invited Filippovskii to attend talks, treating KOCh members at first like returning heroes. Gently it was made clear to them that KOCh would have to be wound up. Voronovich was the first to get a whiff of what lay in store when he was told that, as a military specialist subject to mobilization, he had been drafted into the Red Army and transferred out of the area. Gradually the other KOCh members appreciated that they were under house arrest in the comfort of Sochi's Grand Hotel. They still hoped that when the Bolsheviks called free elections, they would be able to stand. The arrival of the Cheka ended such fantasies. Voronovich had already escaped when the other KOCh leaders were arrested at the end of May.[19]

The Rout of Kolchak

The dilemmas faced by the SRs on the Black Sea coast were precisely those faced by the Green commanders in Siberia. Joint Red-Green cooperation in the defeat of the Whites was nowhere clearer than in the case of Kolchak. Red and Green forces fought side by side to defeat him, and it was actually the SRs who detained him first, before later surrendering him to the Bolsheviks. In the political aftermath of his execution, Reds and Greens worked out a *modus vivendi* which allowed Siberia's SRs to retain a modicum of political influence.

In May the Siberian SRs were instructed by the Central Committee that 'independently and not in solidarity with the Bolsheviks' they should work to overthrow Kolchak. Over the summer preparations began within the newly reconstituted Siberian Union of SRs and its secret Central Bureau of Military Organizations (CBMO) for a policy of what might be termed 'temporary regionalism'. The plan was to remove Kolchak and then call a Siberian Land Assembly at which it was hoped the region's popular representatives would agree to negotiate a truce with the advancing Red Army; once the truce had been established the SRs would establish a separate state authority for Eastern Siberia and the Far East. The latter, it was hoped, would in the short term provide a democratic buffer between the capitalist world and Bolshevism, while in the longer term this democratic entity might develop into the first building block of a new democratic federal Russia as other regional governments were established in areas freed from the Whites, most notably on the Black Sea coast.[20]

The prospects for SR success were enormously enhanced by the divisions which developed between Kolchak and General Gajda. Although this row was partly about Gajda's personal vanity after being demoted in June 1919, it also reflected some residual sympathy on Gajda's part for the democratic ambitions of the Czechoslovak Legion and the democratic and regionalist sympathies of many NCOs in the White Army who had become disillusioned with Kolchak's authoritarian rule. The SR idea of calling a Land Assembly until a Siberian Constituent Assembly could meet, was popular and struck a chord with those politicians still loyal to the old Siberian Regional Assembly dissolved by Mikhailov in 1918. In response they established a 'Coordinating Committee for the Convocation of the Land Assembly' with branches in Krasnoyarsk, Irkutsk and Vladivostok; it was led by the former chairman of the Siberian Regional Assembly. On 5 September it published a charter calling for the overthrow of Kolchak and invited all delegates to the Second All-Siberian Congress of Regional and City Councils, which Kolchak had banned from taking place in Tomsk in May 1919, to assemble in Irkutsk early in October and proclaim themselves the Land Assembly. Only a few managed to make the journey but those who did established a 'council-socialist conference' which agreed to start preparing the necessary apparatus for an anti-Kolchak coup d'etat.[21]

No sooner had these first moves been made, than the issue of cooperation with the Red Army was raised. A group calling itself the Autonomous Group of Siberian SRs decided in favour of close cooperation with the Red Army and broke away from the plotters. The majority rejected this and preferred to look for support to dissident army officers like Gajda and the Allies. The SR plotters were in close contact with the British consul in Vladivostok and believed he would support them. In early September, Gajda advised the British of his plans to become involved in action against Kolchak and on 7 November he informed them that the coup would take place in Vladivostok the moment Omsk fell to the Red Army. As promised, the action duly began on 17 November. Leaflets went out announcing a Provisional People's Government in Siberia, with Gajda at the head of a new People's Army; armistice negotiations with the Red Army would begin at once. Unfortunately for the plotters, they acted prematurely and without any active support from the British. Kolchak's military governor succeeded in restoring control and 500 of the insurgents were executed; Gajda and the former chairman of the Siberian Regional Assembly escaped with Allied help.[22]

However, just before Gajda's move in Vladivostok, on 12 November the Coordinating Committee for the Convocation of a Land Assembly succeeded in summoning sufficient delegates to the Congress of Regional and City Councils in Irkutsk to set about forming a Political Centre whose purpose would be the overthrow of Kolchak and the formation of a coalition socialist government; that government would call for a ceasefire with the Red Army followed by talks to establish regional autonomy. The local Bolsheviks at first supported the formation of this Political Centre, but the Third All-Siberian Bolshevik Conference, also meeting in Irkutsk, was instructed to have no further contact with the Political Centre and withdrew its representatives.

To try and forestall the coup planned by the Political Centre, Kolchak's officials set about trying to give their regime a more democratic façade. Kolchak had already promised in mid-September that he would summon a State Land Assembly; but on 16 November made clear that only one third of the delegates to it would be elected, the other two thirds would be appointed, half of them by Kolchak himself. As the situation worsened, Kolchak promised to reconvene the State Economic Conference, and there was even talk that Kolchak would drop his insistence that one third of the delegates to the State Land Assembly be nominated by him. Yet when the reconvened State Economic Conference opened on 8 December not even the most right-wing SRs were interested in cooperating with it: the right-SR dominated cooperative Zakupsbyt called for an immediate negotiated peace. Kolchak, despite the moves of his officials, showed no willingness to adapt to the new realities and made clear that he would not be convening a Land Assembly after all, not even one dominated by his appointees. With no signs of compromise, the Political Centre prepared for insurrection.[23] They were only too well aware that Kolchak's brutality continued. On 12 November, two days before the Red Army took Omsk, the authorities shot all those political prisoners detained in the local prison.[24]

As Kolchak's retreating army approached Irkutsk, the plans were already well advanced. On 24 December, with the support of locally garrisoned Czechoslovak troops and the local Bolsheviks, despite the instructions they had received from Moscow, an insurrection took place in the railway station suburb on the far side of the river Angara from the city centre. With the insurgents in control of the station and Kolchak's forces still controlling Irkutsk city centre a ceasefire was brokered by the Allies. Under its terms the Political Centre would

A train wrecked by Bolshevik action, Siberia, 1919.

agree to let Kolchak and the Whites pass through Irkutsk and on past Lake Baikal to Vladivostok; in return Kolchak would pass his gold reserves to the Political Centre which, once Kolchak was at a safe distance, would open cease-fire talks with the Bolsheviks. This ceasefire soon broke down, sporadic fighting resumed on 27 December, and by 2 January 1920 it was clear that the Political Centre was getting the upper hand. When the Whites took advantage of a second Allied brokered ceasefire to bring up reinforcements, fighting resumed on 4 January and the insurgents, now describing themselves as the People's Revolutionary Army, assumed power in Irkutsk the next day. Detained by the Czechoslovaks in Nizhneudinsk, Kolchak was returned to Irkutsk on 15 January to stand trial.[25]

The Irkutsk SR insurrection was mirrored by an SR planned revolt in Krasnoyarsk, which broke out on 25 December.[26] However far from all the non-Bolshevik forces opposing Kolchak were linked to the SR's People's Revolutionary Army. As Kolchak retreated, it was Green partisans who took Tomsk in September 1919 and Slavgorod in November. Some of these forces adopted the title People's Army, others, like the 16,000 strong Altai Peasant Red Army, had no affiliation to the SR party; but when they spoke of Soviet power they had in mind soviets dominated by the peasants rather than the Bolsheviks. Typical of their views was a declaration adopted in Minusinsk which, for all the references to soviet Russia, stressed SR slogans like proportional representation in elections, guarantees of freedom of speech, press and the individual, and the formation of a united socialist front. Estimates of the strength of such units vary greatly, but in Western Siberia there were from 140,000 to 175,000. Most were happy, after Kolchak's defeat, to be turned into reserve units of the Red Army; attempts to disarm them, however, were not always successful, suggesting an ambiguous political stance.[27] In mid-February the local Red Army commander in Chelyabinsk, a former Left SR, was accused of being unwilling to take firm action against armed detachments organized by his one time party comrades.[28]

The Political Centre, like Filippovskii's KOCh, at first thought it would be able to stand up to the Bolsheviks. During its brief tenure of office in Irkutsk, from 7 – 21 January 1920, its members pursued the twin goals of democracy and regional autonomy. One of those involved it its activities was the same Zionist who had met Avksentiev in Tomsk on 15 November 1918. Inspired by what he later described as 'a lovely plan, built on sand', he took a post in the Political Centre's Foreign Ministry, where he busied himself studying papers seized from Kolchak's files.[29] Although on 22 January 1920 the Political Centre agreed to cede power in Irkutsk to a Bolshevik sponsored Revolutionary Military Committee, matters did not end there. While making concessions over the future of Irkutsk, the SRs revived in parallel the notion of regional autonomy further east. The SRs proposed the formation of an autonomous People's Republic in Siberia and the Far East.

This proposal, advanced by the SR Central Committee, was at the heart of talks which began in Tomsk on 19 January between the Bolsheviks and the Political Centre. Progress was slow. The initial talks broke down and resumed in Krasnoyarsk on 24 January. A disagreement developed about where the borders of the state should lie. The Bolsheviks, who had accepted the formation of the state in principle, were adamant it should be east of Lake Baikal, something initially the SRs refused to accept since the loss of Irkutsk would mean their state would have no coal industry worthy of the name. A White counter-attack stalled the talks process in February – a counter-attack which prompted the summary execution of Kolchak on 6 February – but after the Red Army arrived in Irkutsk on 6 March the talks resumed. When the SRs tried again to raise the question of territory, Lenin took a firm line: if his views were not accepted, the SRs should be arrested. By 6 April it had been agreed to establish a Far Eastern Republic comprising the provinces of Pribaikal, Zabaikal, Amur, Primore, Kamchatka and North Sakhalin. The capital moved from Verkhneudinsk (Ulan Ude) to Chita in October 1920. It was far from all the SRs had wanted or were anticipating, but it kept alive the notion of a democratic federation of Russian states. As far as the SRs were concerned, the Bolshevik retention of power remained tenuous, and the possibility of rebellions peasants forming other autonomous republics was very real.[30]

On the other hand, it was equally clear that the Bolsheviks had found a potent method of asserting their political hegemony through the Red Army. The Siberian partisans who accepted their new status as reserve units of the Red Army had to obey orders. Makhno and Voronovich were both called on by the

Red Army to recognize the authority of the Red Army's High Command, which at the same time meant they had to subject themselves to the political control of the Bolsheviks. Many of the independent Green units fighting alongside the Red Army in autumn 1919 recognized the military logic of a close association with Trotsky's HQ; the attitude of the PoW regiments among the Black Sea Greens was probably typical. Among many rank and file Greens the logic of war suggested they should defeat the Whites and then think about the future under the Bolsheviks. As more far sighted Greens like Makhno and Voronovich realized, such feelings were already being manipulated by the Bolsheviks to their own ends. Thus military discipline was regularly used to limit political dissent. If military discipline could be used to impose political orthodoxy, the Bolshevik leaders believed in spring 1920 that it could also be used to build socialism.

Labour Armies and World Revolution

To all intents and purposes the Russian civil war seemed over by early 1920. However, as their attitude to Makhno, to the Black Sea Greens and to the Siberian SRs made clear, the Bolsheviks did not see victory as the occasion to cede political power. Lenin had already made clear that the tactic was not to share power with peasant parties but to change the Bolsheviks' peasant policy. By spring 1920 the concessions to the middle peasantry were consistently applied; there was no more talk of communes or Poor Peasants' Committees. Yet the formation of communes had been only one part of the problem as far as peasants were concerned. Constructing state farms and communes involved depriving peasants of their land and that could never be acceptable to the peasants. However, wooing the middle peasantry did not mean ending the policy of forcing peasants to accept low prices for arbitrarily requisitioned grain. Grain requisitioning would never be popular with the peasantry, but in spring 1920 it remained an essential part of Bolshevik economic policy.

Victory over Kolchak and Denikin induced in the Bolsheviks an extraordinary mood of triumphalism. Forgetting the role played by Makhno, Voronovich and the Siberian SRs in the defeat of the Whites, the Bolsheviks immediately resumed what they saw as the pressing task of building socialism. As far as they were concerned, the same techniques which had won the war could now be used to win the peace. Spring 1920 saw the formation of so-called 'labour armies'. From mid-January onwards the government set about rebuilding the country through a complex hierarchy of labour armies which were seen as moving the country one step further away from the bourgeois money based economy and one step nearer socialism: as was noted by those trying to form a labour army in Siberia 'the Revolutionary Labour Army is a first step towards creating a socialist economic organism for the region'. Military units, instead of being demobilized, were transferred into armies of workers, still subject to military discipline and military rations, which were deployed to carry out crucial reconstruction work. The detailed plans of these labour armies, however, show that one of their main tasks was 'to collect systematically all surpluses', in other words to collect grain. Convinced that administration could supplant the market, the commanders of these armies were, according to Trotsky, 'to forward to their superiors precise operational labour reports, stating the quantity of grain collected, loaded and transported, the number of cubic metres of firewood felled and cut up, and all other work'. The country was to be run through a paper chase of such operational reports.

The enthusiasm for socialist construction was linked as before to a renewed expectation of imminent world revolution. At the end of January 1920 Red Army communists were told to prepare for action, since a new wave of international revolution was about to begin. The defeat of Denikin had opened up two new fronts, as the Bolsheviks saw it. First in the south, where Bolshevik control of the north Caucasus would mark the end of Menshevik Georgia and secure communist power in Azerbaijan. From there it would be possible to mount a challenge to British imperialism in Persia; in May 1920 the short-lived Soviet Republic of Gilan was indeed established in north Persia. Second, Denikin's defeat opened the way to re-establishing soviet control in Bessarabia and from there the prospect of revolution in Romania.[31]

As things turned out it was Soviet Russia's border dispute with Poland, rather than the issue of Bessarabia, which reignited the prospect of world revolution. After a series of border incidents and skirmishes with Poland during 1919, which had resulted in the loss of Vilna and Minsk, followed in January 1920 by the loss of Dvinsk and in March 1920 by the loss of Mozyr, the Bolshevik government decided to try to retrieve the situation and ordered Budyenny's First Cavalry Army to deploy from the south to the Polish border. Before it arrived the Polish Army launched a major offensive against Soviet Russia on 25 April, taking the Red Army by surprise and pre-empting, so the Poles hoped, any Bolshevik dreams of spreading revolution to the borderlands with Poland. The Polish advance was dramatic and by 6 May they had taken Kiev, but thereafter their plan backfired badly. The western frontier had been only lightly defended and, despite the speed of the Polish advance, the Red Army had not been surrounded or cut off. As it retreated it prepared for a counter-offensive.

Budyenny's First Cavalry Army launched that counter-offensive on 30 May and successfully turned the front. Kiev was retaken on 12 June; a month later Minsk was captured on 11 July, followed by Vilna on 14 July and Brest Litovsk on 1 August; by the third week of August the Red Army was fighting on the river Vistula and Warsaw seemed to be about to fall. Moscow was suddenly gripped by a tumultuous wave of revolutionary enthusiasm. At last everything seemed to be happening as Lenin had predicted. The Second Congress of the Communist International had opened in Petrograd on 19 July and continued until 7 August. Delegates could hardly believe that all the privations of years of underground struggle were about to be vindicated. A map was pinned to the wall to display the Red Army's daily progress, and the second session was delayed to allow Lenin time to return to Moscow to supervise the war effort. Lenin was convinced that this time world revolution was imminent and pushed to one side the caution being expressed by those commanding the Red Army, Trotsky and Stalin. Allied proposals for mediation were cast aside.[32]

Lenin's revolutionary war did not turn out as planned. The Red Army was defeated on the Vistula and thereafter forced into a steady retreat which continued until, on 12 October, an armistice was negotiated; the armistice was consolidated as the Treaty of Riga in March 1921.

Defeating Wrangel

The Bolsheviks were forced to abandon their dreams of revolution and negotiate with their enemies not only because the Poles fought back, but because the Russo-Polish War enabled General Wrangel to launch the last desperate campaign of the White Generals. With Allied help, Denikin's White Army had overcome the harrying tactics of the Black Sea Greens and escaped to a safe refuge on the Crimean peninsula. There Denikin had resigned and been replaced as White commander by General Wrangel, the captor of Tsaritsyn. On 6 June 1920 Wrangel's forces left the Crimea, where he had given an undertaking to the Allies to remain, and advanced onto the Tauride plain. He soon won control of north Tauride, reaching as far as the river Dnieper and within a fortnight he had doubled the territory under his control. At the end of June Red Army units hastily diverted from the Polish front tried to counter-attack, but they were ill-prepared and the attack rapidly turned into a disastrous rout with the loss of 3,000 horses. A month later, in early August, the Red Army tried again and this time, after the bitterest of fighting, a successful bridgehead was established at Kakhovka fifty miles north of Perekop. Here trenches were dug and the fighting resembled that of the First World War; not even Wrangel's British tanks gave him a decisive advantage. Yet, despite this setback, the initiative remained with Wrangel.

On his other front, the Dnieper front Wrangel continued to make modest gains. He took Aleksandrovsk (Zaporozhe) to the north and Mariupol (Zhdanov) to the east in September and early October. On 6 October he launched a massive offensive and succeeded in crossing the Dnieper. For a week bitter fighting followed, but on 13 October he was forced to retreat back across the river. This military turning point coincided with the political one. The armistice with Poland was signed on 12 October and by the end of the month Budyenny's crack cavalry forces were ready to use against him. The Red Army's offensive began on 28 October with Budyenny advancing seventy five miles from Kakhovka towards the railway linking Wrangel's forces to the Crimea. However, the other Red forces moved more slowly and although the Whites lost one hundred guns, seven armoured trains and 20,000 prisoners, or sixty per cent

Red artillery in action during the fighting with Wrangel, Kakhovka, August 1920.

of their forces, the elite regiments were able to retreat across the Perekop isthmus back into the Crimea. Here the Red Army was helped by the weather. On 7 November, the third anniversary of the Bolshevik seizure of power, the weather was so cold, and the wind so strong, that the Sivash salt sea partly dried out and partly froze, allowing the Red Army to cross behind the Whites and launch a surprise attack. There were more decisive battles on 10-11 November, but on 14 November Wrangel boarded ship for exile.[33]

However, as at every stage of the Red-White struggle, the Greens were involved in this final stage of the civil war. Unlike Kolchak and Denikin, Wrangel had a clear land policy. Before launching his break-out in June he announced a land law which would distribute the large estates to the peasants, while offering compensation to the former landlords. Perhaps for this reason he was hopeful of establishing a working relationship with Green forces. On 8 August Wrangel landed 4,500 men on the Kuban coast in an effort to seize Krasnodar and breath new vigour into the Kuban Cossacks. After three weeks, however, the remnants of that army re-embarked for Crimea having singularly failed to open up a second front. Wrangel had hoped his path to the Kuban Cossacks would be smoothed by Voronovich's Green forces. However, Wrangel had misread the situation disastrously. After the arrest of Filippovskii, Voronovich, thoroughly disillusioned with Bolshevik rule, had returned to the mountains. There he had established a new partisan force with a new General Staff and which, in line with his long held strategy had established contact with

A supply convoy provisioning Red troops during the Wrangel campaign.

the Kuban Cossacks. The plan was, as before, to organize a joint insurrection of Green partisans and Kuban Cossacks. Voronovich, who remained loyal to his SR convictions, refused to have anything to do with Wrangel and a strategy that would link the Kuban Cossacks to the Whites. Wrangel's Kuban adventure was frustrated by Voronovich.[34]

At the start of his campaign Wrangel had tried sending a similar emissary to Makhno. Despite the fact that he had been hounded by the Red Army since January 1920, Makhno shot Wrangel's messenger on the spot. Instead, in July and again in August Makhno proposed to the Bolsheviks that they should cooperate in a joint action against Wrangel; the Bolsheviks responded in September. Talks were held in Kharkov at the moment when the Wrangel threat seemed at its greatest: the Bolsheviks met Makhno's representatives between 10-15 October when the armistice negotiations with Poland had still not been concluded. An agreement was hammered out which had two sections, a military agreement and a political agreement. The first was relatively uncontroversial: the Insurgent Army would come under the operational control of the Red Army, while retaining its own internal structure; subsequent clauses prevented the Insurgent Army from recruiting deserters from the Red Army and accepted that any isolated Red Army men who had ended up with Makhno would be returned to their original units. The political agreement, however, was more controversial.

The political agreement covered the release of all Makhnovist prisoners and guaranteed anarchists complete freedom of speech, publication and agitation in the soviets. The most controversial clause, clause four, stated that in Insurgent Army controlled areas workers and peasants would be allowed to elect their own soviets which would later federate to the Soviet Government. It was reminiscent in this respect of SR policy. Not surprisingly the Kharkov Bolsheviks were unwilling to publicize this agreement. At the end of the talks they agreed to publish the military agreement, but the political agreement would have to be endorsed by Moscow, they said. It never was. The Bolsheviks realized that they had panicked. With the Polish armistice secured on 12 October the defeat of Wrangel was bloody but relatively straight forward. The Insurgent Army loyally played its part in the campaign but no sooner had Wrangel embarked for a life of exile on 14 November than, on 23 November, the agreement with Makhno was broken. Makhno was ordered to integrate his forces fully with the Red Army. When he refused, on 26 November, the Red Army attacked the Insurgent Army. Ironically, this assault was justified by reference to clause four of the political agreement, still unratified by Moscow, which Lenin chose to interpret as an attempt to prepare for an insurrection; its implementation would certainly have ended soviet power as Lenin understood it.[35]

Green Rebellion

The Bolsheviks' Green critics had repeatedly stated that, once the Whites were defeated, they would turn their attention to the Reds. They were as good as their word. From autumn 1920 until spring 1921 the Bolsheviks faced a Green rebellion throughout Russia. Primarily through the efforts of the SRs, Unions of Toiling Peasantry, the SRs' political 'third force', were created in Tambov, Voronezh, Saratov and Samara provinces. By April 1921 165 large peasant insurgent detachments were active in Russia, of which 140 had clear SR orientation. In Siberia the powerful Peasant Union, also led by the SRs, coordinated peasant insurrections in Omsk, Tyumen, Chelyabinsk and Ekaterinburg provinces involving 100,000 participants.[36] Although the origins of these insurrections were usually spontaneous, sparked off by a particular incident of Bolshevik high-handedness, as the insurrections took hold they became increasingly organized and echoed the politics and policies developed first by the Directory and then revived on the Black Sea by KOCh and in Siberia by the Political Centre.

Makhno led the Green rebellion in Ukraine. For a further nine months after the Red Army turned on him he tried to keep alive the notion of direct soviet democracy. During winter 1920-21 he and his 3,000 men were steadily driven west towards Kiev, fighting daily, but avoiding major confrontations. Spring 1921 found him, now deprived of all artillery, executing an erratic march from Kiev towards Galicia, then back to Kiev and eastwards again to Poltava and

Kharkov, then north toward Kursk and Belgorod, before heading south again towards Ekaterinoslav and the Tauride province by March. Mostly these sudden changes of direction were simply dictated by his Bolshevik pursuers, but occasionally he responded to the requests of peasant delegations to visit their region. As long as he could, he continued with the cultural-educational section of his Insurgent Army and distributed his *Statutes of the Free Soviets* wherever he went; he was always revived by resolutions like those received from Chernigov peasants in summer 1921 calling for the formation of 'free soviets'. Although nearly wiped out in April 1921, by May his strength was back up to 2,000 men and serious plans were drawn up to attack Kharkov. In June a strike-bound Ekaterinoslav was rocked by rumours that Makhno was about to seize the town; in preparation his supporters cut the telegraph wires but before they did so a message was broadcast to all soviets demanding new elections to 'free soviets'. As the Red Army prepared more and more assiduously for his annihilation, the reality of his plight was catching up with him. Forced to move east towards the Volga below Tsaritsyn, he then passed through the Don, towards the Sea of Azov and finally ba ck across the Dnieper, where, at the end of August 1921 he decided to flee abroad.[37]

As during 1919, the Bolsheviks were terrified in 1920 that Makhnovism might prove to be infectious. As Budyenny's Red Cavalry was moved from the Polish Front to confront Wrangel there was worrying evidence of disaffection. As early as 1 September a report described the mood among some cavalrymen as 'demoralized by counter-revolutionary elements'. It went on:

> Since the earliest days when the units started to move, in certain groups within the Sixth Division a feeling started: 'Let us purge the rear of Jews. Let's go and join Bat'ko Makhno. Let's live without commissars and communists.'

A month later, on 3 October, it was reported that the same division had refused to take orders from their commander and were 'proceeding to the rear areas with the slogans 'Kill the Jews, communists and commissars; Save Russia'; the soldiers quoted Makhno as the leader who had given them that slogan.'

Such contact with Makhno must have been by repute, rather than the consequence of direct talks since Makhno was determinedly opposed to anti-semitism; however the slogan against communists and commissars was genuine enough. On 6 October 1920 Trotsky was informed of other such incidents in a report which concluded:

> New evidence has confirmed information previously reported concerning the counter-revolutionary mood in parts of Budyenny's army. Although that information was undoubtedly exaggerated there is nevertheless a good deal of truth in it. Since Makhno is in the area of the front and there is inevitably some contact between

his units and ours, the above-mentioned information about Budyenny's army assumes special significance. This must be taken into account, even though there can be no doubt about Budyenny's own position and devotion to Soviet power.[38]

On 10 October 1920 dissident cavalrymen were involved in a pogrom against Jews and communists, resulting in thirty deaths and several burnt houses; a prison was also broken open. Reviewing the mood among the cavalrymen after Wrangel's defeat a party commissar noted that he still frequently heard the slogan 'we'll finish of Wrangel and then finish of the commune', and that, although currently absorbed in military activities, 'if there is another long period of quiet all these anti-Soviet, anti-communist forces will show up again'. And they did. In May 1921 the former head of the First Brigade of Budyenny's Fourth Cavalry joined Makhno and organized a short-lived insurrection on the Don.[39]

Given the Makhno danger, the Bolshevik authorities decided to take pre-emptive action against the Don Cossacks' former hero, Mironov. After the victory over Denikin, Mironov had been given a pen-pushing job in the Cossack section of the soviet apparatus, carrying out routine administrative tasks and occasionally losing his temper about cases of bureaucracy and maladministration. When the Wrangel crisis broke, he volunteered for service and was appointed to command the Second Cavalry Army. However, in December 1920 he was one of those detailed to pursue Makhno, and the Red Army leadership began to suspect that Mironov was showing a certain softness towards his quarry. He was summoned to Moscow on 4 December. Not long after this, on 18 December, a relatively small scale Cossack insurrection broke out on the Don, organized by K.T. Vakulin, one of Mironov's former commanders. To make matters worse, Mironov had not gone straight to Moscow when summoned, but had stayed on in the Don area. On 20 January 1921 he was relieved of his post and given family leave before a new assignment.

When Mironov returned to his native Ust-Medveditskaya on 8 February 1921 he was accompanied by a Cheka spy who not only reported on Mironov's understandable bitterness at the way he was again being marginalized, but interpreted his actions at a meeting with a small group of confidants in Mikhailovka as the start of preparations for an insurrection which would seek to restore 'popular power' (*narodovlastie*). Although it seems that the spy misrepresented Mironov's actions, and that Mironov actually tried to dissuade his friends from premature insurrection, they did discuss at length the need to purge the soviet administration of bureaucrats and restore the soviets to something like their original 1917 structure, when they had indeed come close to representing 'popular power'. That was dangerous enough; Mironov was arrested on 13 February 1921 and shot in secret in April.[40]

The brutal execution of Mironov was essential from a Bolshevik standpoint because unrest on the Don could open a vital link between the Green movement of Makhno in Ukraine and the other huge peasant rebellion of autumn 1920, that of Aleksandr Antonov. Indeed, when Mironov's erstwhile associate Vakulin rebelled, the crux of his appeal was precisely that: he told his followers that, if he could win the support both of Mironov and Budyenny – something he clearly anticipated achieving with little difficulty – a link could be established between Makhno and Antonov. Vakulin claimed in this appeal that Antonov had already marched as far towards the Don as Borisoglebsk and had captured the town.[41] If it had been vital for the Reds to prevent Denikin and Kolchak linking up, it was equally essential to prevent the Green peasant insurgents doing the same.

Despite the execution of Mironov and the crushing of the Don as a bridgehead between Antonov and Makhno, there were attempts at cooperation, at least on Makhno's part. At the beginning of March 1921 he formed a group which set off to enter the Voronezh region. In summer 1921, just before his flight abroad, he made two further efforts to broaden his activities. In August two of his commanders were sent on raids across the Volga, which ultimately proved unsuccessful. Not long before this Makhno had even tried sending forces further afield. He recalled in a letter sent when in exile how he had formed a unit of 'former Siberians' and sent them under the command of a certain Comrade Glazunov to make contact with sympathizers in Siberia. They were last heard of fighting in Samara province at the beginning of August 1921.[42]

Antonov's rebellion remained isolated from Makhno's Insurgent Army, but it was in many ways more impressive, both in scale and scope. Based on a core of military supplies confiscated from the Czechoslovak Legion in May 1918, Antonov eventually built up a Partisan Army of 20,000 men formed into mounted regiments of 300-500 men each; these core troops were sometimes supported by a further 30,000 ill-armed peasants. Antonov's campaign lasted until June 1921 and for most of that time only the towns and railway lines of Tambov province remained under Bolshevik control. The insurrection began as so many others had done. It was prompted by the arrival of a grain requisitioning detachment in the village of Kamenka, south east Tambov province. Since this was the second visit to the same village by such a detachment, the peasants protested and their protest was supported by the local branch of the SR sponsored Union of Working Peasants. An ugly scene ensued and seven members of the Bolsheviks' requisition brigade were killed. To protect themselves from the violence of a government punishment brigade, the peasants formed themselves into an armed unit which successfully repulsed three visits by punishment brigades. Chance then intervened. A provincial conference of the Union of Working Peasants was taking place at that time and was persuaded by Antonov to turn this incident into a wider protest; the conference delegates agreed to do so largely because the Cheka had started to arrest any member of the Union of Working Peasants who discussed the Kamenka incident. By 21 August the area was under martial law.

Antonov's relationship with the SR Party was far from straight forward. In 1920 he described himself as an 'independent SR': in pre-revolutionary times he had been a militant member of the party, taking part in a number of bank raids to raise funds; during autumn 1917 he had sided with the Left SRs. However, disillusioned by the Left SR connivance in the dispersal of the Constituent Assembly, he broke with the party just before the Left SR July insurrection in 1918 and thereafter he kept a certain distance from both its wings. Yet from spring 1920 he threw himself wholeheartedly into the SR sponsored campaign to build the Union of Toiling Peasants into a non-party organization which could challenge the Bolshevik monopoly of power and it was around the Unions of Toiling Peasants that his rebellion was organized. In May 1920 Antonov was instrumental in organizing a Tambov Region Conference of the Union of Toiling Peasants, which adopted a programme calling for the overthrow of the communist dictatorship, the socialization of the land, and the summoning of a new Constituent Assembly; to this end partisan units were to be formed and retained until that assembly met.

The SR Party had no problem with the formation of the Union of Toiling Peasants, for it was part of their third force strategy, an organization for promoting legal political struggle against the Bolsheviks. On 17 February 1920 the SR Central Committee had informed party organizations by letter that the tactic of relying on the peasantry to create a 'third force' seemed to be working. In May 1920 Chernov had expressed the view that in this context the Union of Toiling Peasants had a special role to play in areas of the country under soviet control; he called on them to organize meetings to try to force the local soviet authorities to submit to a vote of confidence. Nor did the SR leadership oppose in principle the idea of an insurrection. However, they did doubt whether the time for an insurrection was right and whether Antonov was the man for the job. Eventually they disassociated themselves from his actions. In July 1920 the Tambov SR conference warned Antonov not to establish partisan units. Antonov took no notice and in September after the insurrection had begun he again ignored a call from the All-Russian SR Party Conference in Moscow to call off his armed action. Central Committee condemnation was repeated on 26 February and 26 April 1921, although the Voronezh South Eastern Regional Committee of the SR Party meeting on 28 April 1921 voted to support him. The Left SRs were fully behind Antonov and since the formation of Unions of Toiling Peasants was a joint SR-Left SR undertaking in which both parties tried to establish parity representation, at local level Antonov inevitably collaborated with both wings of the SR Party. Indeed in some places in Tambov Province the two wings of the party had fused.[43]

The most striking thing about Antonov's campaign was its high level of organization. Antonov had been a driving force in the movement to establish the Union of Toiling Peasants before the insurrection began, and used these contacts as the core of his rebellion; at the height of his campaign, January 1921, there were over 900 village branches of the Union of Toiling Peasants.[44]

Antonov's control of this organization was total. Initially some of the regional committees of the Union of Toiling Peasants were ambivalent towards Antonov's campaign; he supplanted these doubters with a three-man provincial committee which strongly supported him.[45] In mid-November Antonov called a meeting of all his commanders and established clear command structures for military and political life. This established a Main Operations Staff headed by Antonov and along side it a 'Political Bureau' responsible for agitation work among the army and also for managing the civilian police force. By the time of a further conference in late December 1920 the Union of Toiling Peasants had requisitioned buildings for its local and provincial offices, established its own courts, launched a campaign against home distilled vodka, brought all flour mills under popular control, fixed certain wages and drafted a policy for feeding and equipping its army. Running such a large territory through a system of directly elected peasant unions was similar to the formation of peasant soviets in 1917 and the practical reality of the slogan 'soviets without communists'.[46]

Until January 1921 the Bolsheviks had relatively few troops in the area, and clearly hoped the situation might right itself. Thereafter, when over 1,000 communists had been killed by Antonov's men overwhelming force was used. Initially the Red Army tried a policy of partial amnesty for those Greens who surrendered and during April 1921 Antonov came under some pressure from within the Union of Toiling Peasants to seek a negotiated settlement. Antonov was determined to resist to the bitter end. He retook the territory the Bolsheviks had gained through their amnesty policy and when the Red Army resumed its offensive in May and June terror was the order of the day. The Red force of 50,000 men took control of the area and over 600 hostages were shot and a minimum of 30,000 people exiled. Antonov himself was only tracked down a year later and shot in a final skirmish.[47]

Antonov's rebellion was far from unique. The continuation of grain requisitioning in spring 1920, the era of the labour armies, had caused widespread unrest even before Antonov's insurrection began. In Ufa and Ekaterinburg provinces there had been disturbances in February 1920, while in May, in the Altai region of Siberia, a former partisan leader in the struggle against Kolchak had organized a rebellion against the Bolsheviks under the slogan 'hail anarchy, the mother of order'. In mid-July 1920 a former Left SR serving as the Red Army's military commander for the Lower Volga Military District imitated Muraviev by arresting the local communists and starting a rebellion which soon spread through Samara, Saratov, Tsaritsyn and the Urals, before being suppressed in September 1920.[48] Of these other peasant rebellions, however, the most significant was that which began in Western Siberia in early 1921.

Towards the end of September 1920 the Bolsheviks in Tyumen Province decided that peasant surpluses existed in many areas of their region. At a series of meetings organized by the Siberian Peasants' Union peasants resolved that, while they were not opposed in principle to requisitioning, they could only fulfill demands made which were 'within the bounds of possibility'. By the end of October anti-Bolshevik pamphlets were circulating widely, and throughout the winter many local soviet leaders tried to prevent the activities of the requisitioning units; from November 1920 to February 1921 nearly 100 local soviet leaders were arrested on this charge. At this stage the struggle was peaceful, and very often led by women. They would declare the village soviet dissolved and form in its place a 'women's soviet', which would then petition the higher authorities to remove the grain requisitioning detachments. What turned these peaceful protests into violent ones was the Bolshevik decision to launch yet another requisitioning campaign in spring 1921. For most peasants this went beyond the bounds of what was possible. On 31 January in a village north of Ishim, peasants tried to prevent a requisitioning brigade from leaving with its booty; soldiers opened fire killing two peasants, and, armed only with pitchforks, the peasants drove out the brigade.

As in Tambov province, so too in Western Siberia the insurrections very soon became highly organized. Sending couriers to nearby villages the revolt spread rapidly. Soon the whole of north Ishim was affected and by mid-February one million square kilometres of territory was lost to soviet control. For three weeks the Omsk-Moscow telegraph was cut, as were the railways via Chelyabinsk and Ekaterinburg. On 14 February 1921 the town of Petropavlovsk was captured for a few days but Tobolsk was held by the rebels for six weeks. Because of the sheer size of the area covered the movement was more spontaneous than that of Antonov. Men were formed into divisions, groups and armies of the self-proclaimed People's Army, but they operated more or less autonomously; thus the Ishim People's Army existed alongside the Tobolsk People's Army. However, a complex system of couriers, reporting twice a day, did ensure some coordination. For the time they controlled Tobolsk a new democratic Peasant-Town Soviet was elected, headed by a leading member of the cooperative movement and this body chose an executive of eighteen and established various sub-committees; the paper *The Voice of the People's Army* appeared daily from 27 February to 7 April. Similar initiatives were undertaken where ever the rebels won power: new soviet elections were held, civil rights restored, the class basis for rationing abolished and free trade established. In Western Siberia there were clear echoes of the Komuch administration of 1918 both in the establishment of a 'war industries committee', to provide for the needs of the 'People's Army', and in the decision to fly the red flag and sing the Marseillaise. In Siberia soviets without communists really were being established.

The insurgents of Western Siberia were very conscious of the fact that they were not acting alone. *The Voice of the People's Army* carried regular stories of peasant insurrections in other parts of the country, seeking to put the events in Tobolsk in the broader context of a peasant war which would ultimately drive the Bolsheviks from power. And practical moves were taken to bring this about. Just as Makhno had tried to establish contact with Antonov, so the rebels on the Volga tried to make contact with the West Siberian insurrection. A thousand strong band from the Volga tried to march to Siberia but was trapped near Chelyabinsk in June 1921 and eventually forced to retreat. By then, however, the insurrection was past its peak. After bitter fighting throughout the second half of March between Ishim and Tobolsk the Red Army succeeded in retaking Tobolsk on 8 April; it took a further month before the leaders of the insurrection were captured and even longer before the area was secured, but the Volga mission came too late to retrieve the situation.[49]

The New Economic Policy

On 2 February 1921 the Bolshevik Politburo met to discuss the worsening crisis, with the situation in Tambov at the forefront of their minds. At this stage there was no suggestion of a radical change in policy, just emergency relief for some peasants and emergency repression for others. However, throughout February events moved with accelerating speed. On 8 February however Lenin presented the Politburo with his 'Preliminary Rough Draft Theses Concerning the Peasants': this stood Bolshevik policy on its head since it conceded the demand for a 'firm' grain price, something for which radical SRs had been campaigning since summer 1918. Lenin proposed in the place of grain requisitioning a tax in kind at a level lower than the previous year's procurement target, to be linked to free trade in grain beyond that tax threshold. He distributed copies of his paper to a working party and called for a report within a fortnight. Meantime on 12 February grain requisitioning was abolished in Tambov province and on 14 February Lenin received a delegation of carefully chosen Tambov peasants. On 16 February *Pravda* published the views of those both for and against Lenin's paper, while on 18 February a draft decree was produced by that arch-conciliator Kamenev; this was endorsed by the Central Committee on 24 February. Lenin's plan was clearly to get the Tenth Party Congress to endorse the new policy when it met early in March, and the delegates were given a hint of the way things were going by a *Pravda* story on 28 February which described how the authorities in Ishim had executed the leader of a requisitioning brigade for exceeding his powers.[50]

By the time the Tenth Party congress opened on 8 March there was no time for the luxury of debate. During the last week of February and the first week of march the Bolsheviks' hold on the monopoly of political power became increasingly tenuous. With the war against Poland over workers were determined there should be no return to the Labour Armies of the spring. A labour revolt, which had been building for some months, exploded in February 1921. Sparked off by a cut in the ration, widespread strikes hit Petrograd, Moscow, Saratov, Ekaterinoslav, the Donbas and the Urals. In Petrograd these strikes were near general by the third week of February, and what worried the authorities most was that they were organized by Mensheviks and SRs; the core of the unrest in the capital was the Trubochnoi Zavod, one of the first factories to join the Assembly of Factory Delegates in 1918. The situation was so serious that the Bolsheviks had to deploy troops in the city to prevent strikers demonstrating on the streets and thus spreading their message further; the frozen river Neva, however, meant that strikers could dodge the bullets and cross from one industrial suburb to another.[51]

This labour unrest coincided with the anarchist-led rebellion of the garrison of the island naval base at Kronstadt, which defended Petrograd from the sea. Since the end of February the Kronstadt garrison had been refusing to obey orders; on 2 March it arrested the Bolshevik commanders and commissars and called for free elections to the soviets, with freedom of speech and press for anarchist and socialist parties. It was 18 March before the Red Army had crushed the mutiny, two days after the closure of the Tenth Party Congress; as this book's cover shows, the Red Army had to suppress the rebels by attacking across the frozen waters of the Gulf of Finland, suffering many casualties. The Kronstadt mutiny was the straw which broke the camel's back. The Tenth Party Congress agreed to accept Lenin's paper on a tax in kind as the basis for a complete overhaul of economic policy. By the summer the New Economic Policy would be in place. If that were the cost of retaining power, the Bolsheviks would drop their socialist offensive and introduce a pro-peasant policy. The Green rebels had fought the Bolsheviks to a sort of stalemate. There would be no concessions concerning the Bolsheviks' claim to a monopoly of political power – those Red Army soldiers who died putting down the Kronstadt mutiny were given heroes' funerals – but after the mutiny the Bolsheviks were prepared to pursue an economic policy acceptable to the peasant majority of the population.

FIVE

Red Victory: Causes and Consequences

The Tenth Congress of the Bolshevik Party and the introduction of Lenin's NEP marked the end of Russia's civil war. The economic changes introduced then brought about a reconciliation of sorts between the Bolsheviks and the peasantry; as a consequence peasant unrest died down. The Bolsheviks had retained their monopoly of power, they had won. They had won partly because they had turned the Red Army into an effective fighting force, but also because of the weaknesses of their opponents and the success of the Bolsheviks in exploiting those weaknesses. The Whites had no social policy, no coherent policy towards the land, and so could be portrayed, and did in fact behave, like those wishing to restore the Tsarist past. The Greens were not so easily ridiculed but they were perpetually divided. Whether the radical SRs called themselves Left SRs, Borotbists, Maximalists or the Narod Group, they were constantly at loggerheads with Right SRs, or indeed some of Makhno's anarchists, about what sort of deal, if any, could be struck with the Bolsheviks. After the October coup of 1917 the Bolsheviks had agreed, under popular pressure, to form a coalition government with the Left SRs; it did not seem so out of the question that they might be persuaded to do so again. This seemed to many SRs a more realistic expectation than that of the extreme Right SRs who were never certain whether the future really lay in a close alliance with the Allies.

The Bolsheviks were not magnanimous in victory. Economic concessions were one thing, political concessions something else entirely. As Lenin had said when abandoning the Poor Peasants' Committees in December 1918, it was a question of the Bolsheviks changing their policy in order to retain power. The SR political leaders were hounded to the point of extinction, as were the anarchists. The Bolsheviks' dream of world revolution might have been put on hold, but the Bolsheviks were determined that their political dictatorship should continue until the prospects for that revolution revived. During the civil war the Bolsheviks had learned the art of ruling in the face of mass political hostility. Those methods would not be forgotten when during Stalin's collectivization campaign it was decided to settle scores with the peasantry once and for all.

The Red Army

At one most basic level, the Whites were defeated because, by the end, the Red Army outnumbered the White forces by a ratio of five to one.[1] The growth in the size of the Red Army was astonishing. During December 1918 it increased from 372,000 to 435,000; by mid-1919 it had reached over 1,500,000.[2] For the crucial counter-offensive against Denikin and the victory at Kastornoe, the Red Army mobilized every last man. Between 1 September and 15 November 1919 100,000 new soldiers were sent by the Red Army to the Southern Front. Apart from a continuing deficiency in cavalry, the Red Army had overwhelming superiority: it had 160,000 infantry, 26,000 cavalry and 4,500 machine guns while Denikin had 63,000 infantry, 48,000 cavalry and 2,300 machine guns. For the final assault on Wrangel, even the deficiency in cavalry had been rectified. In October 1920 the Red Army's infantry outnumbered Wrangel's by more than four to one, the cavalry by three to one, and artillery by two to one. Only in terms of tanks, armoured trains and planes was there anything like parity.[3]

It was not simply a question of size or the correct balance of infantry and cavalry. When, after the Bolsheviks' conquest of Sochi, Voronovich, the commander of the Green forces on the Black Sea Coast, came out of the hills to discuss the future relationship between his forces and the Red Army, he encountered Red Army officers and men for the first time since 1918. He was, he recalled, astonished by their discipline and military bearing. The Bolsheviks, he concluded, had turned the Red Guard rabble of 1918 into a mass, educated fighting force which was better than the pre-revolutionary Imperial Army. When he went to meet the new Red Army commander at Sochi he was amazed at the reception he was given. After being led in by a batman, the Red Army commander introduced himself and clicked his spurs, before cordially inviting Voronovich to sit down. After their talk, he was invited to take tea with the commander's wife. It was just like under the old regime.[4]

Trotsky would have been proud that his army could be compared favourably with that of the Tsar. It had always been his ambition to create just such an army. In the process, however, he had had to overcome much opposition. Suspicion of former Tsarist officers was endemic among the Bolsheviks; the behaviour of Muraviev on the Volga front in July 1918 was a constant reminder that loyalty could not be assumed. Keeping the army loyal meant establishing a Bolshevik core within it. And, although the growth in the size of the Red Army's party organization was remarkable, it could not keep pace with the growth in the army itself. Thus, early in 1918 there were 115,000 party members; early in 1919, 251,500; and early in 1921, 585,600[5]: between March 1918 and March 1920 the total party membership in the Red Army rose from 45,000 to 300,000, although, of course, many members died on the battlefield. The number of party cells rose from 3,000 at the end of 1918 to roughly 7,000 by mid-1920.[6]

Party control over the Red Army was exercised through the system of political commissars which the Bolsheviks inherited from the former Provisional Government. The system took a while to establish, for in the immediate aftermath of the Bolshevik seizure of power many party members saw the election of officers and the formation of soldiers' committees as more appropriate forms of political control. These were abolished in decrees passed in March and April 1918. Trotsky wanted a professional army. In article after article he defended the use of military specialists from the old Imperial Army and insisted that officers' orders had to be obeyed. Having established that the Red Army would be controlled by a system of Bolshevik commissars, and not rank and file soldiers, these questions then arose: who appointed the commissars and what were the respective rights and powers of commissars and commanders? Commissars were to be appointed by the Bolshevik Party, but at what level? To sideline interference from local party activists who might try to develop practices which would politicize the officer corps, in June 1918 all party cells in military units were separated from their territorial links to the local town party organization and put under central control; by October 1918 this meant being under the control of political departments which were directly subservient to the Central Committee. Trotsky faced opposition to the formation of such Political Departments from within the Red Army officer corps, delaying implementation from October to December 1918, while also infuriating many in the Bolshevik by downgrading the powers of the commissars themselves. Commissars were responsible for political work, not operational matters; it was commanders who controlled troop movements.[7]

There were many in the Party who felt this arrangement reflected Trotsky's enthusiasm for military specialists which for many had gone beyond all bounds during the fighting for Kazan in August and September 1918. When Trotsky arrived in Sviyazhsk to restore order after Muraviev's rebellion, he insisted not only on giving his new commanders enormous powers but deliberately downgraded the status of the commissars. He demanded that all those responsible for the rout, commissars as well as commanders, should be punished. In an infamous judgement Commissar Panteleev was sentenced to death for agreeing to a retreat ordered by his commanders. To the Party at large this was outrageous: if Commissar Panteleev had had the power to countermand the orders issued by the officers, the judgement and death sentence might have been justified, but Trotsky's management of the Red Army meant that he had no such power. Panteleev, a loyal communist, was being treated like his counter-revolutionary officers. Shooting a party member was too much for many communists, and Stalin soon became a mouthpiece for those Bolsheviks worried about Trotsky's policy.[8]

As preparations began for the Eighth Party Congress in March 1919 Trotsky faced much criticism of his military policies. There was widespread dissatisfaction with the high salary levels Trotsky had agreed to pay officers and the small number of officers from proletarian backgrounds; but the crux of the matter was the limited authority of the commissars vis-à-vis the commanders, particularly since rumours abounded that Trotsky planned to increase the power of commanders still further. Stalin was among those critical of Trotsky's plans, largely because of his own experience of former Tsarist officers. At the end of September 1918 he had protested when the High Command tried to impose a new commander for the Southern Front based at Tsaritsyn. The proposed commander Stalin felt was politically suspect. In this row Stalin was supported by his long time associate, Voroshilov. It took a month and all Lenin's undoubted diplomatic skills to smooth over this clash. Stalin was moved to the heart of politics in Moscow, while the amour propre of the Red Army was upheld by the new commander first taking up his post and then being quietly transferred to other duties.

The fall of Perm in December 1918 provided Stalin and those critical of Trotsky's policies with a further opportunity to push home their case. Stalin was, as has been shown, one of those on the investigating team sent to establish why this crucial strategic centre had put up so little resistance. His commission established that the main military reason for the fall of Perm was that, with insufficient reserves, the Red Army had been forced to mobilize local peasants; however, the loyalty of those peasants to the Bolshevik regime, given the Bolsheviks' agrarian policy was minimal and they simply deserted. Stalin's commission of enquiry encapsulated this as the adoption of 'pre-revolutionary training methods' which reflected the 'counter-revolutionary spirit' surrounding the Supreme Red Army Commander Vacietis. These findings were toned down in the final version of the report on Perm's capture, but they clearly reflected Stalin's views. A truly 'red' commander would have had a 'class attitude' towards whom to mobilize. At the very least, if workers were not available for conscription, Vacietis should have tried to ensure that the hurriedly mobilized peasants were given some ideological training.

When the Eighth Party Congress met in March 1919, Trotsky's line, supported by the Central Committee, was subjected to severe criticism and the delegates' military commission voted against the stance of the Central Committee. Stalin, associated with the opposition but loyal to the Central Committee, played a crucial role in resolving the crisis and rallying waverers to support the leadership. In the final congress resolutions the powers of commissars were subtly increased: operational matters were still beyond their control, but their powers were broadened. Henceforth they had a duty to organize mass party meetings, even at the front; they were given the authority to arrest those considered disloyal; and they were put in charge of the security departments. In these and other ways the principle that party members should play a greater role in running the army was endorsed and a balance of power between commissars and commanders established which would remain without significant change until the Second World War.[9]

It would be quite wrong to paint too rosy a picture of the Red Army, however. For all the spur clicking of Voronovich's Red Army commander once the war was over, the war was, like any war, depressingly brutal; heroism was a scarce commodity. Campaigns could be ill-thought through and pointless. When the Red Army launched an assault on the Donets river in spring 1919 only the 23rd Rifle Division of the Ninth Army managed to get across to the far bank, losing 2,000 men as prisoners, drowned or killed in the process. With no units in reserve, and the only supporting units still on the original side of the river, the division faced a force six times its size. After beating off five attacks, without food or sleep for four days, they had to retreat across the river, with many more drowning on the return journey. In the aftermath of the operation, in early May, the men were without footwear or clothing for several weeks; in one regiment 600 men were bare foot. In the desperate struggle to stop Denikin's advance 'we took people from the fields and work shops, gave them no uniform or boots, and put them in no cohesive military units, and threw them at the front', a report stated on the fighting in May 1919. Even six months later, when Denikin was in full retreat an observer commented on how badly the care of the wounded was organized: 'the men who came out of the line had to drag themselves along for several miles before they could get a first dressing for their wounds'.[10]

Many of the military casualties were victims of disease rather than glorious engagements on the battlefield. Disease affected both sides. However, a survey carried out in August 1919 to discover the reasons for the Red Army's spring retreat revealed that the dramatic collapse on the Southern Front was accentuated by a typhus outbreak. The author of a report included in the survey noted:

> When I arrived with the Ninth Army at the start of April I was horrified at what I found – barracks, hospitals, shelters overflowing with victims of typhus. For every division of six regiments (and if the division had three brigades then there were nine regiments) there was one or at best two doctors, and the regimental 'coolers' were being used as a medical unit. Not only were there no doctors, but no medical orderlies and no nurses. On a tour of inspection I asked about medicines, but everywhere the picture was the same; there were no medicines and any bandages had to be re-used repeatedly. This was taking place when the Chief Health Officer could report that he had ample supplies.

There then followed a frantic effort to evacuate the 'dying army', loading stretchers on and off boats and across rickety pontoon bridges. Although the Chief Health Officer for the Southern Front refused to talk of an epidemic, in April 1919 between 30 and 40 men were dying every day in regiments numbering 400 to 500 men. This had a devastating impact on fighting capacity. By mid-May the Ninth Army was so depleted it faced an enemy twice its size with four times as many cavalry.[11]

Despite the enormous stress given by Bolsheviks to political work in the Red Army it remained patchy to a degree. Party work often quite simply collapsed. On the Southern Front in February 1919 it was reported that there were no political commissars. By the spring most units would have a small body of party members and sympathizers, but when it came to action enormous drive was needed to overcome objective difficulties. A party activist recuperating from typhus decided to organize a literacy class; he could get no books nor pencils. Even for those who could read, the newspapers rarely arrived on time, usually with a delay of two weeks but sometimes as long as a month. Even in November 1919 when the Red Army was functioning well, a report stressed how rare newspapers were and how hard it was to find good party workers. Reports showed that on the Southern Front political work was very patchy, with some politically conscious units complete with functioning comrade courts and others where the commissars themselves were clearly make-weight. However the very fact that there was a Political Department which expected such reports to be sent in regularly had an impact; political work, even at a patchy and primitive level, was carried out. When communist activists and sympathizers dodged military action and failed to play the leading role required of them, reports on such incidents were forwarded via a hierarchy of committees to the Central Committee of the Bolshevik Party itself.[12]

Where military and political leadership were poor, desertion could become a major problem. A report of August 1919 noted tension within one unit stationed on the Southern Front between the commander, who had once served at the Tsar's GHQ, and his rather lacklustre commissar; the result was poor political work, problems with the conscripted peasants of Saratov province who were described as 'extremely unreliable' and a large number of desertions. To address the problem the Red Army established an Anti-Desertion Commission. In July 1919 on the southern front a provincial Anti-Desertion Commission reported detaining 30 deserters a week; they had assembled 150 to be shipped to rear. By December 1919 the Central Anti-Desertion Commission made clear that there would be no let up in its campaign even with victory in sight. The following categories of people were to be considered deserters: 'all those who without authorization absent themselves from military units, factories, institutions and enterprises, when the staff of same have been declared as mobilized by decrees of the Defence Council, those who overstay any sort of leave, and those who do not report when mobilized'. Not only those who deserted but those who harboured deserters or knew of their whereabouts would be dealt with. In this last category special responsibility was laid on the chairmen of local house committees and local councils. Nevertheless, in January 1920, in the closing stages of the war, Trotsky was alarmed by a report which suggested that in some front line units 75 per cent of troops were deserting.[13] With as many as 200,000 men deserting each month from July to December 1919 it has been estimated that the total number of desertions was 1.5 million.[14] Desertion was often to Green units rather than to the White cause, but such a distinction was quite unacceptable to the Bolsheviks. The anti-desertion campaigns only ever posed the stark choice of Red or White, producing posters like *Plate 1*. The work of Vasilii Spasskii in 1919, the poster shows exploited peasants being liberated by the Red Army, but victory is short-lived because of desertion and the symbols of the old order return. In Bolshevik propaganda there was no third way.

Winning Hearts and Minds

The Bolsheviks defeated the White generals because, in the end, they were able to mobilize more of the population to their side. Ultimately they could do this because the Whites failed to develop a land policy, or any coherent social policy, and preferred the symbols and slogans of the old regime. In areas controlled by the Whites, the absence of any sort of progressive social programme was brought home to the population by the shear brutality of White rule. In areas under Bolshevik control this message was not so self-evident and had to be put across by propaganda. The Bolshevik Party devoted considerable energies to propaganda, persuading many of the country's most famous artists to commit themselves to the war effort in this way. The easiest propaganda message to get across was that the Whites represented the old order: *Plate 2*, the work of Victor Deni in 1919, shows Kolchak's imperial ambitions, his brutality and his links to the bourgeoisie, the church and, allegedly, the kulaks. The slogan makes clear that the land and the factories were to be returned to the capitalists and land-owners, while the gallows are reserved for workers and peasants. Another of Deni's works, *Plate 3*, gives essentially the same message: the slogan on the flag reads 'shoot every tenth worker and peasant'. The same theme is adopted by Deni in *Plate 4* when denouncing Denikin. Dmitrii Moor's appeal for Wrangel to be crushed without mercy before he reconquered the Donbas, *Plate 5*, has Denikin, Yudenich and Kolchak rising from the bowels of the earth.

Using propaganda to attack the Bolsheviks' enemies was only half the story. Explaining Bolshevik policy was the other half, and explaining Bolshevik grain policy to a sceptical peasantry was not easy. The Party's approach was two-fold. First those peasants who refused to supply bread to the Red Army and towns had to be demonized as kulaks. Kulaks often appeared in the list of the regime's enemies, but it was important not only to show the kulak standing beside the former landlords, but to single out the rich peasant as a blood sucker, who cared nothing for those around him. In 1920 Vladimir Lebedev depicted the classic image of the alleged kulak, *Plate 6*; while the poor peasant is on the brink of starvation, the kulak sits with his bottle, his joint of meat and his bourgeois aspirations represented by the gramophone. The other side of the coin was the positive Bolshevik message: grain fed the Red Army and the

Red Army would defeat the Whites and thus prevent the return of the landlords. This message was given graphically in *Plate 7*: 'if you do not want to end up feeding the landlords, you must feed the Red Army', the message reads. A similar stark choice is depicted in *Plate 8,* a poster drawn by Dmitrii Moor in 1919. Specifically aimed at the Cossack, it asks whether the Cossack soldier in the centre is with the Red Army on the left, or the White band on the right.

The most difficult message the Bolsheviks had to get across was their attitude to the Greens. Early in 1920 *Red Soldier*, the newspaper of the 3rd Infantry Rifle Division fighting in the south, published a report entitled 'The Green Army'. Conceding that 'comrades are greatly interested in the Green Army', it stressed the difference between the Green forces of Voronovich, fighting for Soviet power and against Denikin, who 'are our friends' and the bands of deserters and kulaks in the rear who had dodged the call-up, lived by banditry, and used slogans such as 'long live the soviets, down with the communists!'. The identification of even some Green forces as progressive was uncharacteristic, and, of course, only some of Voronovich's forces were ready to cooperate with the Red Army while others followed Voronovich himself back into the mountains for a further spell as a 'bandit' leader.[15]

The *Red Soldier* article concluded that most Greens were traitors and 'defenders of the old gang of landowners and bourgeois', and *Plate 9*, an anonymous poster, makes the same point, but for the SR Party rather than Greens in general. It makes clear that behind the SRs stood the forces of the old regime: the text refers to both Mensheviks and SRs, but the flag bears the slogan 'Land and Freedom to the People', the traditional cry of the SRs; the man carrying the flag fits the Bolshevik stereotype of the SRs, a student radical out of touch with the realities of life. The SRs are depicted in a similar manner in *Plate 10*; produced in 1920 this Vladimir Lebedev poster portrays the SR as a typical intellectual, out of place in the village: the text neatly sums up the SRs' dilemma in 1919-1920; it reads: 'Ask an SR what does he believe, he'll tell you land to the peasants, but the peasants to whom? – to the English'.

This line of reasoning was effective. The defeat of the SRs and the Green forces associated with them was not simply the result of oppression, of the force used to crush the rebellions of Antonov, Makhno and others. There was another compelling reason why many on the Green side should be unwilling to continue an armed struggle against the Reds once the Whites were defeated. Ever since the end of the First World War, as Lenin noted in his *Speech to a Moscow Party Workers' Meeting* on 27 November 1918, patriotism had worked for the Bolshevik side. 'History has veered round to bring patriotism back to us', Lenin noted. He went on: 'Up until now the petty bourgeois [i.e. the peasants] had cherished the illusion that the British, French and Americans stood for real democracy'.[16] The post-war behaviour of all three powers in abandoning the Directory and supporting first Kolchak and then Denikin had soon crushed that illusion.

In his seminal essay *The Valuable Admissions of Pitirim Sorokin* Lenin stressed that in this new situation the SRs would divide into three blocks; some would support the Bolsheviks; some would stay neutral; and some would drift towards the Allies. He was correct. From 1917 to 1921 the SR Party remained divided. On the left, the Left SRs, Ukrainian Borotbists, the Narod Group and the 'front delegation' among the Black Sea Greens all accepted the need for some sort of collaboration with the Bolsheviks. On the right, the Siberian SRs were prepared to look to the Allies, as was Voronovich on the Black Sea. The decision of the centrist SR Filippovskii not to back Voronovich's plans to defend a Green redoubt against the Red Army was symptomatic of the way in which most SRs ultimately resolved their dilemma. Filippovskii felt that, with Denikin's defeat in sight, there was no need to confront the Bolsheviks with force of arms; they would listen to reason.

The problem for the SRs in those dying days of the civil war, when they were still articulating plans for a new Russia based around a federation of states, democratic in Siberia and the Black Sea but soviet in central Russia, was this: it was easy for the Bolsheviks to portray these plans as anti-patriotic. The Bolsheviks went out of their way to stress that such a future was only possible with Allied support. This was difficult to challenge. It was clear that the Black Sea Greens had benefitted from the continued existence of British-supported Menshevik Georgia, while in Siberia at least some of the Allies, despairing of Kolchak, had opted for encouraging the SRs. Thus the impact of the 'Ask an SR what does he believe in' poster. Its slogan summed up the dilemma faced by Russia's Greens. Presented with the choice between a Bolshevik dictatorship or a White Guard authoritarian regime, the SR third way was bound to look attractive; but on closer inspection the SRs were divided between those prepared to strike a deal with the Bolsheviks and those looking to external support.

Revenge on the SRs

The Bolsheviks' Tenth Party Congress not only introduced NEP as a concession to the peasantry, it firmly established Soviet Russia as a one-party dictatorship. Although the Mensheviks and SRs were not formally excluded from the soviets as they had been in June 1918, their organizations were persecuted to the point of extinction. Any political activity resulted in arrest. Not even the Narod Group was allowed to operate freely. A Cheka circular of 1 June 1920 concluded that the group was nothing less than a legal cloak for the illegal core of SR members who still supported Chernov and his policy of a 'third force'. Although later that year the Cheka grudgingly admitted that members of the group had tried to persuade rank-and-file party members to express loyalty to the Soviet regime, it was clear to the Cheka that the Narod Group's aim in persuading party members to accept the Soviet state was to obtain a base from which to construct a powerful revitalized political party capable of opposing the Bolsheviks from within the soviet political structure; to this end they inevitably made what the Cheka interpreted as 'inadmissible criticisms' of current government policies and attempted to take advantage of the difficult situation in the country 'to win over the petty bourgeois strata of the population'. The Narod Group continued to operate until spring 1922 under the leadership of Volskii, but another founder member Burevoi left in protest at the attitude of the Cheka in February 1922. Many Narod Group members concluded that, if cooperating with the Bolsheviks only led to Cheka persecution, there was little point in remaining separate from the SR Party proper. Many therefore responded to an appeal by Chernov in July 1921 to rejoin the mother party.[17]

As to the SR Party itself, the majority of its Central Committee was arrested in the first half of 1920 as soon as victory over Denikin had been achieved. Many of those active in the Komuch administration, like its one time foreign minister Mikhail Vedenyapin, were also arrested at this time. With the detention of the Central Committee an ad hoc Organizational Bureau led the party from June 1920 to August 1921, after which further arrests led to the formation of a five-member Central Bureau. In September 1920 ten delegates attended a conference in Moscow and in August 1921 a final Tenth Party Council was held in Samara. The party activists who managed to attend these illegal gatherings tended to be far more radical than the imprisoned members of the Central Committee and on both occasions the resolutions adopted clashed with the views of the imprisoned Party leadership. In October 1920 Vedenyapin condemned the implicit support given by the September Conference for armed insurrection against the Bolsheviks, while in September 1921 the Central Committee sent a letter from prison again making clear that the party could not support partisan style insurrections as the resolutions of the Tenth Party Council seemed to imply.[18]

Despite such exaggerated caution on the part of the SR leadership, the Bolsheviks decided on 28 December 1921 to put the surviving leaders of the SR Party on trial. Those tried *in absentia* included the party leader, Chernov, two of the SR members of the Directory, Avksentiev and Zenzinov, and the leader of the Archangel Government, Chaikovskii. Those put on trial in person included right-wingers, like Likhach, who had been arrested along with the members of the Directory during Kolchak's coup, as well as Centrist SRs associated with the Komuch administration like Vedenyapin. Among the witnesses brought from their prison cells to speak up for the defence were Filippovskii, leader of the Black Sea Greens; Volskii and Burevoi, the founders of the Narod Group; Rakitnikov, a leading member of the Komuch administration; and Dedusenko, a member of Chaikovskii's Archangel Government. One of the defence counsels was G.B. Patushinskii, the SR who had served for a while as Justice Minister in the Siberian Government in summer 1918 when he had been a vociferous critic of Mikhailov.[19]

The purpose of the trial was clear from the start, to try to persuade SR party members to break with the organization by showing its 'true' face. When the trial opened in the first week of June 1922 a great deal of effort was spent trying to prove that, at a time when the SR Party's actual concern was the Komuch People's Army and its bitter clash with the Red Army for control of Kazan, the SR Central Committee had found time to endorse the attempt by Fanny Kaplan to assassinate Lenin on 30 August 1918. While it was clear that leading SRs, among them some of the defendants, had known of Kaplan's plans, the Party leadership had never endorsed this terrorist act. The Bolsheviks were equally determined to prove the close contacts which had existed between the SRs and the Allies, ignoring the fact that the party had been deeply split on this issue and that the relationship between the SR Central Committee and the Union for the Regeneration of Russia had been particularly fraught (it was, after all, only the URR and not the SR Central Committee which had established any formal link with the Allies). Finally, the Bolsheviks accused the SRs of having organized the Tambov rebellion, when it was quite clear that the SR Central Committee had infuriated its own party rank and file by refusing to encourage armed action against the Bolsheviks and had publicly disassociated itself from Antonov.[20]

However, this was a show trial and the charges of terror, betrayal and insurrection were 'proved'. The accused were duly convicted early in August; their pleas – that the Bolsheviks, not the SRs, had been responsible for the outbreak of Russia's civil war and that only History could be their judge – were simply ignored. At first the Bolshevik Central Committee wanted to impose the death penalty but Kamenev, architect of the Railway Workers' Union talks, the February 1919 amnesty, and the May 1919 meeting with Makhno, persuaded his comrades to back down; the death sentences originally passed were commuted to terms of imprisonment on condition that the SRs cease their underground and terrorist activity. The trial was followed by a campaign to persuade the party rank and file to break with the past; this culminated in March 1923 with an All-Russian Congress of Ordinary SRs, attended by forty-five delegates representing 850 members, which formally wound up the SR Party. A year later it was reported that 2,000 people had declared themselves 'former SRs', but given that at its peak the party had several hundred thousand members this was small beer. The last underground Central Bureau was arrested in 1925.[21]

Early Stalinism

The Stalinist state was formed in the crucible of Russia's civil war as the Bolsheviks fought both to defeat their opponents and retain their monopoly of political power. The second of these concerns was more central than the first, when it came to creating a Bolshevik political culture. What really formed the future Stalinist state were the civil war confrontations between the Bolshevik Party and the population at large. These confrontations, which produced a series of crises that had clear parallels with the events of the 1930s, were prompted by the attempts, made from the moment of the break with the Left SRs in spring 1918, to 'build socialism'. In April 1918, Lenin had called for the complete nationalization of the Russian economy and issued his *Six Theses on the Immediate Tasks of the Soviet Government*, endorsed by the Central Committee early in May. These linked the idea of state accounting and control to the introduction of one-man management and increased labour productivity through the use of Taylorism, planning and labour discipline, all policies which the working class rejected. The result was labour unrest, especially in Petrograd, where the Menshevik- and SR-sponsored Assembly of Factory Delegates was soon wielding tremendous authority. Only the arrest of the Assembly leaders prevented a city-wide strike in the first week of June 1918.[22]

This assault on workers was only part of the story. Lenin concluded his *Six Theses on the Immediate Tasks of the Soviet Government* with 'a general and summarizing slogan of the moment – iron discipline and the thorough exercise of proletarian dictatorship against petty-bourgeois vacillation'. By petty-bourgeois Lenin meant peasants and their political voice, the SRs. So began the Bolshevik campaign to establish Poor Peasants' Committees, which in turn prompted the Left SR insurrection and the associated peasant insurgencies of the summer and autumn of 1918. For the Bolsheviks to keep control of key cities in the summer of 1918, amid a sea of peasant insurrection and worsening labour unrest, it was essential to appoint ruthless officials to maintain order. Stalin was himself given this task in Tsaritsyn. Early in June 1918 Stalin had been appointed as General Director of Food Affairs in South Russia and sent to Tsaritsyn. In August the local Cheka uncovered an alleged conspiracy by SRs and ex-officers, the aim of which was to rally a local unit of Serbian PoWs to follow in the footsteps of the Czechoslovak Legion and rebel against the Bolsheviks in order to reopen the Eastern Front. One of the major conspirators detained was a so-called 'bourgeois specialist', the railway engineer N.P. Alekseev. As far as the local Cheka were concerned, 'all specialists are bourgeois and most are counter-revolutionary'; Stalin seems to have thought the same way. Alekseev was arrested and shot. Perhaps of more significance for the future than Alekseev's execution, for there was some plausible evidence against him, was the way in which Stalin scooped up in the investigation a number of those merely on the fringes of the affair, but who Stalin suspected of opposing him. The only crime of one of the people caught up in this way had been to complain to Moscow about Stalin's highhanded behaviour.[23]

Another key strategic town for Bolshevik survival in summer 1918, as the clashes between the Red Army and the People's Army began, was Nizhny Novgorod. Situated on the river Volga, but relatively close to Moscow, it was a key centre for grain collection. The man sent on 26 May 1918 to retain it for the Bolsheviks was one of Stalin's most trusted supporters, Lazar Kaganovich, who would later become the figurehead of those opposed to Khrushchev's destalinization policies in the 1950s. His immediate task was to keep control of the city as the Mensheviks and SRs organized a Conference of Representatives of Factories and Works in Nizhny Novgorod and Vladimir Provinces, which took place on 10 June and was attended by over 200 worker delegates. Kaganovich's initial response – to send in Red Guards who would disrupt its opening – backfired and by 18 June the massive Sormovo works was on strike, with most city centre shops closed down in sympathy. No sooner had this strike been put down and order restored than Kaganovich had to face down the Left SRs, who vehemently opposed what the Bolsheviks liked to term the 'food supply dictatorship'. When the Left SRs threatened to leave the (as they considered it) gerrymandered soviet which ran Nizhny Novgorod, Kaganovich boasted that the Bolsheviks could rule alone. When the Left SR insurrection broke out in Moscow on 6 July, Kaganovich responded by closing down the local Left SR press on 8 July and expelling them from the soviets on the 11th.

With the fall of Kazan to the People's Army, Lenin urged Kaganovich to take even more drastic measures. On 9 August he instructed the local Cheka:

> It is necessary to use all force, to set up a dictatorial troika, to institute immediately mass terror, to shoot and deport hundreds of prostitutes who get the soldiers drunk...

Less hysterical orders came two days later, demanding searches, preventive arrests of former Tsarist officers and members of the bourgeoisie, and the posting of guards to key installations. When Lenin was shot and wounded on 30 August, the authorities in Nizhny Novgorod decided to respond by shooting the 'bourgeois' hostages they had taken. Earlier on the same day Kaganovich had introduced a delegate from the Central Committee to a mass meeting at the Sormovo works. Disappointed by the poor numbers attending, Kaganovich felt the need for force rather than persuasion. As he later reported:

> [When Lenin was attacked] the Provincial Party Committee inspired the Red Terror which was carried out in our province. I will not enumerate how many were arrested and shot but this Red Terror was felt by our bourgeoisie, so that here alone of all provinces there was no incident of counter-revolutionary action. The counter-revolutionary bourgeoisie and kulakdom was absolutely smashed not only here but in the whole province.

The recapture of Kazan early in September eased the immediate crisis in Nizhny Novgorod. Kaganovich, however, stayed on and began to institutionalize his undemocratic rule in ways that would become characteristic of Stalinism. He advised colleagues:

> When the Party Provincial Committee decrees to shoot ten people, you take such a resolution, but it is not you who carry it out; to shoot and arrest is not the business of the Provincial Committee. The Provincial Committee instructs the chairman of the Cheka, who is a member of our party, and he carries it out... The Provincial Committee proposes, but officially the accusation is from the organs of power, the military commissariat or the Cheka.

Although there had been much criticism of the Cheka in the run up to the Eighth Party Congress in March 1919, and leading conciliatory figures such as Kamenev had seriously discussed its abolition, Kaganovich had little time for those who criticized it; he retained the Cheka as an essential aspect of life in Nizhny Novgorod. The local Cheka was led by Kaganovich's future Politburo colleague in both Stalin's and Khrushchev's governments, N.A. Bulganin. The high-handedness of the local authorities in Nizhny was highlighted in an article in *Pravda* in April 1919. This reported an incident in Nizhny Novgorod Province where, under the guise of requisitioning, the local authorities had taken away the peasants' personal belongings, clothing, boots, samovars and so forth. When the peasants resisted an armed detachment was called in to suppress what was described as a kulak uprising. *Pravda* reported that the 'detachment arrived and executed those who were pointed out by the local party organization. The detachment left, but everything remained as earlier.... In one village fifty people were executed in this fashion'.

Pravda could risk reporting such incidents in spring 1919 because the new party line was to win the support of the middle peasants and embarrass those opposed to the policy; nevertheless the story was not invented. The persecution of so-called kulaks had prompted mass defections to the Greens; in April 1919 4,900 peasants were apprehended in Nizhny Novgorod province for Green sympathies. Kaganovich was equally brutal when coping with labour unrest. In spring 1919 another strike broke out at the Sormovo works; the strikers' demand that the Constituent Assembly be recalled showed how persistent SR aspirations could be. Kaganovich responded to such overt signs of continued activity by SRs and Mensheviks by starving the strikers back to work. The plant was closed, ringleaders were arrested, and food rations removed for every day a worker remained on strike. Nevertheless, strikes spread to other nearby factories in April, and by July the Sormovo works was on strike again. In his report for that month, it is scarcely surprising that Kaganovich again highlighted the role of the Cheka in combating counter-revolution and preserving order.[24]

Other of Stalin's close supporters in the 1930s had civil war careers similar to that of Kaganovich. Sergei Kirov, whose assassination in December 1934 was to lead to Stalin's purges, held his first responsible post during the civil war in Astrakhan. Astrakhan was always an exposed outpost of Soviet power. At the end of 1918 the man in charge there was A.G. Shlyapnikov, one of the heroes of underground struggle before February 1917 and a key player in the Bolshevik seizure of power. However, Shlyapnikov, whose underground career had revolved precisely around the correct relationship to be established between city and district party organizations, had broken with the party line over Trotsky's military policy. He still felt that the political departments in the army ought be responsible to the local Astrakhan Party organization not the centre. So Kirov was sent to replace him.

Once Kirov was in charge, he acted just as Kaganovich had done. He established a Provisional Military Revolutionary Committee with extraordinary powers; he went into the factories to justify a cut in the bread ration to workers who were preparing to strike in favour of restoring the free trade in grain; he declared martial law on 7 March 1919; and he then put down by force an insurrection which began on 10 March under the slogans 'Death to the communist commissars!', 'Down with the bread ration!', 'Long live the soviets!', 'Down with the Bolsheviks!', 'Long live the Constituent Assembly!', 'Long live the SRs!'. On 11 March Kirov ordered the summary shooting of these striking workers who he categorized as 'Whiteguard swine'. Order was restored by closing all the factories, with the exception of those working on military contracts, and confiscating ration cards; those workers who wished to eat had to present themselves to their factory and ask for permission to resume work, and through work their rations.[25]

Stalin and his most trusted henchmen cut their teeth in the civil war in areas where they had to confront the opposition of the peasants and the anger of the workers through the judicious use of terror. When in 1928 Stalin was looking for supporters as he prepared for collectivization and his new onslaught on the peasantry, it is not surprising that he looked to those who had already engaged in such a struggle during the civil war. It is clear that during the civil war both Kaganovich and Kirov made extensive use of the Cheka when running their fiefdoms. Equally important was the Red Army's Special Section whose *modus operandi* was revealed in a report of September 1919 which described the work of the Special Section in the Tenth Red Army. The report showed that the retreat from Tsaritsyn in the first week of July had been so chaotic that the river steamer in which the section had been housed had only just escaped in time. Nevertheless the Special Section at once resumed activity and set itself the task of recruiting more informants. Its strength as of 5 September stood at 35 agents, of whom only six or seven were classified as 'capable of undertaking serious counter-intelligence work in depth'. Much of the section's work, of course, was relatively routine such as interrogating prisoners of war. However, between 4 July, the date its operations resumed after the evacuation of Tsaritsyn, to 1 September the Special Section charged six people with spying, three with counter-revolutionary activities, sixty nine with dereliction of duty and three with belonging to White Guard organizations.[26] Albeit it on a smaller scale than in the 1930s an important element of Stalin's informer state already existed in embryo mid-way through the civil war.

The Czech author Jaroslav Hasek, best known for his book *The Good Soldier Sveik*, served for a while as a Bolshevik commissar with the Red Army in late 1918. In his story *The Red Commissar*, he satirized the behaviour of such future Stalinists. Hasek's commissar hero, having been informed that the Cheka was about to investigate his conduct, told the local Red Army commander he had nothing to be afraid of:

> [The commander] gave a meaningful whistle. 'He's got nothing to be afraid of! Have you mobilized the horses? No, you have not. Have you got reservists from the local population? No, none at all. Have you levied a contribution on the town? No sign of it. Have you thrown counter-revolutionaries into gaol? Of course not. Have you found a single counter-revolutionary? Not one. And now tell me one last thing: have you had at least one priest or member of the merchant class shot. No you have not done that either. And what about the mayor of the town? Is he alive or dead? Alive. Well, there you are – and you go on telling me you have nothing to be afraid of! It's a bad look out for you, my friend.'[27]

Russia's civil war marked the start of a period in world history when gentle irony and humanitarian concern was not enough to frustrate the ambitions of political zealots.

Notes

Introduction

1. C. Kennedy-Pike, *Russia and the World, 1917-91* (Arnold, London, 1998). p. 208.
2. Figures calculated from O.H. Radkey, *Russia Goes to the Polls* (Cornell University Press, 1990) p. 18.
3. O.H. Radkey, *The Unknown Civil War in Soviet Russia* (Stanford University Press, 1976).
4. P. Kenez, *Civil War in South Russia, 1919-20: the Defeat of the Whites* (University of California Press, 1977), p. 245.
5. Radkey, *Polls*, p. 18.
6. T. Osipova, 'Peasant Rebellions: Origin, Scope, Dynamics and Consequences' in V.N. Brovkin *The Bolsheviks in Russian Society* (Yale University Press, 1997), p. 172.
7. L. Viola, *Peasant Rebels under Stalin* (Oxford University Press 1996), p. 5.
8. A. Graziosi, *The Great Soviet Peasant War: Bolsheviks and the Peasants, 1917-33* (Harvard Papers in Ukrainian Studies, 1997).
9. N.E Kakurin, *Kak srazhalas' revolyutsiya* (Politizdat, Moscow, 1999) Vol. 2, p. 352.
10. E. Mawdsley, *The Russian Civil War* (Allen and Unwin, London, 1987), p. 286.
11. All these works will be referred to more than once and full references will appear below.
12. For a fuller discussion of these April events, see Geoffrey Swain, *Origins of the Civil War* (Longman, Harlow 1996), pp.15 – 20.
13. See Swain, *Origins*, pp. 20 – 23.
14. The classic account of the July days is A. Rabinowitch, *Prelude to the Revolution* (Indiana University Press, 1968).

1 Red Defeat?

1. The standard account of Kornilov's rebellion is G. Katkov, *The Kornilov Affair* (London 1980). A different interpretation is given in Swain, *Origins* pp. 23-38.
2. For a fuller discussion of the politics of the Preparliament, see Geoffrey Swain, 'Before the Fighting Started: a Discussion on the Theme of the "Third Way"', *Revolutionary Russia* Vol. 4 No. 2 1991 pp. 211-215.
3. V.I Lenin, *Collected Works,* (Lawrence and Wishart, London and Moscow, 1972), Vol. 26, p. 234. The crisis within the Bolshevik Central Committee is described in this author's computer assisted learning package *The*

Bolshevik Seizure of Power produced for the HiDES Project, University of Southampton. The standard account is Alexander Rabinowitch, *The Bolsheviks Come to Power* (W.W. Norton & Co. New York) 1976.

4. For a detailed account of the Railway Workers' Union negotiations, see Swain, 'Before', pp. 215-229.

5. The standard account of the various peasant congresses of autumn 1917 is O. H Radkey, *The Sickle under the Hammer* (Columbia University Press 1963). This also contains an account of the formation of the Left SRs. The formation of the Bolshevik- Left SR coalition government is summarised in John L.H. Keep, *The Debate on Soviet Power* (Oxford University Press 1979) pp. 373-5.

6. For the concept of a 'revolutionary convention', see the Soviet meetings of late December 1917 and early January 1918 reproduced in Keep, *Debate*. Radkey, *Sickle* describes the growing influence of the Left SRs.

7. For the attitude of the SRs to the Constituent Assembly, see Swain, *Origins*, pp. 89-91.

8. This summary is taken from Evan Mawdsley, *The Russian Civil War* (Allen and Unwin, 1987) pp. 19-22 and Bruce Lincoln, *Red Victory* (Sphere, London 1991) pp. 74-88.

9. The definitive study of Bolsheviks opposed to the Treaty of Brest Litovsk is R.I. Kowalski, *The Bolshevik Party in Conflict* (Macmillan Basingstoke 1991). For Muraviev and Antonov Ovseenko, see Geoffrey Swain, 'Russia's Garibaldi: The Revolutionary Life of Mikhail Artemevich Muraviev' *Revolutionary Russia* Vol. 11, No. 2, pp. 64-67.

10. For the attitude of the Left SRs to the Treaty of Brest Litovsk, see R. I Kowalski, 'The Left Socialist Revolutionaries after 1917' in *Revolutionary Russia* Vol. 11, No. 2, p. 6. For George Hill see his *Go Spy the Land* (London, 1932) p. 177.

11. The question of British contacts with Trotsky and the repositioning of the Czechoslovak Legion is discussed at length in Swain, *Origins*, pp. 132-145.

12. The regional soviet elections and the Assembly of Factory Delegates are discussed in detail in V. Brovkin, *The Mensheviks after October* (Cornell University Press, 1987). The attitude of the Baltic sailors is discussed in G. Semenov, *Voennaya i boevaya rabota Partii Sotsialistov-Revolyutsionerov za 1917-18* (Moscow 1922), p. 22. For talk of a renewed coalition government, see Swain, *Origins*, pp. 148-9.

13. For the debate in the Central Committee, see 'Iz arkhivov partii' *Izvestiya TsK KPSS* No. 4 1989, p. 141 et seq. For the talks with Germany, see Richard Debo, *Revolution and Survival* (Liverpool University Press 1979), pp. 218-222.

14. The mutiny of the Czechoslovak Legion and the formation of the People's Army is discussed in Swain, *Origins*, pp. 156-160, pp. 167-172.

15. The formation of the Union for the Regeneration of Russia and its links with the Allies are discussed in Swain, *Origins*, pp. 160-167, pp. 172-175.

16. For the Left SRs' tactics at the Fifth Congress of Soviets, see M. Philips-Price, *My Reminiscences of the Russian Revolution* (London, 1921), p. 314. For a detailed discussion of the insurrection, see L Hafner, 'The Assassination of Count Mirbach and the "July Uprising" of the Left SRs in Moscow, 1918' *Russian Review* Vol. 50 1991.

17. The rebellion of Muraviev and the attitude to it of Latvian units on the Kazan front are discussed in Swain, 'Muraviev' and Geoffrey Swain, 'The Disillusioning of the Revolution's Praetorian Guard: The Latvian Riflemen, Summer-Autumn 1918' *Europe-Asia Studies* Vol. 51, No. 4, 1999.

18. For a full discussion of how Allied representatives responded to the shifting loyalties of the Larvian Riflemen, see Geoffrey Swain, "An Interesting and Plausible Proposal": Bruce Lockhart, Sidney Reilly and the Latvian Riflemen, Russia 1918' *Intelligence and National Security* Vol. 14, No. 3, 1999.

19. The outlook of the Komuch administration is discussed in detail in Swain, *Origins*, pp. 187-193.

20. The formation of the Siberian Government is described in detail in J. Smele, *Civil War in Siberia* (Cambridge University Press 1996), pp. 13-33. Details on the early career of Mikhailov can be found in M.A. Novomeysky, *My Siberian Life* (Max Parrish London 1956) p. 165, p. 269.

21. Novomeysky, *Siberian Life*, p. 274.

22. The state conferences in Chelyabinsk and Ufa are discussed in detail in Swain, *Origins*, pp. 193-196, pp. 201- 204, pp. 220-225.

23. The Archangel events are discussed in Swain, *Origins*, pp. 205-214.

24. The Novoselov murder is described in detail in Smele, *Siberia*, pp. 40-44.

25. The early difficulties of the Directory are discussed in Swain, *Origins*, pp. 229-232.

26. Relations between Mikhailov and the Directory are discussed in Swain, *Origins*, pp. 232-234.

27. The dispute between the Directory and the SR Party Central Committee is discussed in Swain, *Origins*, pp. 234-241.

28. Brovkin, *Mensheviks*, p. 282.

29. Leo Steveni, *From Empire to Welfare State*, p. 10/5. This unpublished manuscript, the memoirs of Leo Steveni, was kindly made available to me by his daughters Elizabeth (to whom it is dedicated) and Barbara.

30. Swain, 'Disillusioning', p. 683.

31. Novomeysky, *Siberian Life*, p. 281.

32. D.F. Rakov, *V zastenkakh Kolchaka: golos iz sibiri* (Paris, 1920), p. 293.

2 Red Victory?

1. Smele, *Siberia*, p. 59, p. 97, p. 100.

2. The appeal to President Masaryk is in the State Archive of the Russian Federation (GARF) fond 144, opis 1, ed. khr. 20. Otherwise, Smele, *Siberia* p. 163.

3.   Smele, *Siberia* pp. 164-167.
4.   Smele, *Siberia*, p. 109, pp. 168-179.
5.   Smele, *Siberia*, pp. 195-197.
6.   Smele, *Siberia*, p. 110.
7.   This summary is taken from Smele, *Siberia*, pp. 123-132, p. 151, p. 257, p. 265, pp. 504-5. For White recruitment policy see also N.G.O. Pereira, *White Siberia: the Politics of Civil War*, (McGill-Queen's University Press Montreal 1996) p. 117 and p. 135.
8.   For Cromie, see Swain, 'A Plausible', pp. 83-97; for British recognition, see Swain, *Origins*, p. 245.
9.   Quoted in Smele, *Siberia*, p. 204.
10. Quoted in Smele, *Siberia*, p. 96.
11. Smele, *Siberia*, pp. 116-117.
12. Smele, *Siberia*, p. 141, pp. 336-60; for the massacre of 500 railway workers, see Pereira, *White Siberia*, p. 117.
13. Smele, *Siberia*, p 335 p. 364, pp. 394-412.
14. Kolchak's attitude to the cooperatives is discussed in detail in Smele, *Siberia*, pp. 431-449.
15. Pereira, *White Siberia*, p. 126, p. 136; the land question is discussed at length in Smele, *Siberia*, pp. 274-289.
16. Vladimir Brovkin, *Behind the Front Lines of the Civil War*, (Princeton University Press, 1994) p. 27.
17. These talks are discussed fully in Brovkin, *Behind*, pp. 40-45.
18. Brovkin, *Behind*, p. 33, p. 55, pp. 72 et seq.
19. The debate about the future of the Cheka is given in Brovkin, *Behind*, pp. 45-56.
20. Brovkin, *Behind*, p. 53, p. 55.
21. Lenin, *Collected Works*, Vol. 28, pp. 185-194.
22. Lenin, *Collected Works*, Vol. 28, pp. 201-224.
23. Lenin, *Collected Works*, Vol. 28, p. 118.
24. Lenin, *Collected Works*, Vol. 28, p. 143.
25. Lenin, *Collected Works*, Vol. 28, p. 175.
26. Lenin, *Collected Works*, Vol. 28, pp. 338-347.
27. Lenin, *Collected Works*, Vol. 28, p. 364.
28. Lenin, *Collected Works*, Vol. 44, p. 173, p. 174, p, 181.
29. Lincoln, *Red Victory*, p. 384; Brovkin, *Behind*, p. 31.
30. Pereira, *White Siberia*, p. 115.
31. Pereira, *White Siberia*, p. 123.
32. J.V. Stalin, *Collected Works* (Moscow 1954), Vol. 4, p. 219 et seq.
33. Smele, *Siberia*, p. 187, p. 218.
34. The nature of Khanzhin's army is discussed in Smele, *Siberia*, p. 325; for the executions and peasant unrest, see Brovkin, *Behind*, p. 93, p. 100.
35. Smele, *Siberia*, pp. 316-20.
36. The rise of Green partisans in Siberia is discussed in Pereira, *White Siberia*, p. 144 and the same author's 'The Partisan Movement in Western Siberia,

1918-20' *Jahrbuecher fuer Geschichte Ost-Europas,* 1990, No. 1, pp. 89-90; for a contemporary account, see K. Burevoi, *Kolchakovshchina* (Moscow 1919), pp. 29-30.

37. Brovkin, *Behind*, p. 199, p. 201.
38. The revival of the State Economic Conference is discussed in Smele, *Siberia*, pp. 504-516.
39. This summary of events in the south is drawn from Mawdsley, *Civil War*, pp 85-98. The figures for British aid are on p. 167.
40. V.P. Butt et al., *The Russian Civil War: Documents from the Soviet Archives* (Macmillan Basingstoke 1996), p. 43.
41. Mawdsley, *Civil War*, pp. 163-166.
42. The formation of the Latvian Soviet Republic is discussed in James D. White, 'National Communism and World Revolution: the Political Consequences of German Military Withdrawal from the Baltic Area 1918-19', *Europe-Asia Studies*, Vol. 46, No. 8, 1994.
43. For the formation of the Ukrainian Soviet Government, see A.E. Adams, *Bolsheviks in the Ukraine: the Second Campaign, 1918-19* (Yale University Press 1963). This summary comes from chapters two and three.
44. Brovkin, *Behind*, p. 38.

3 White Victory?

1. P. Stuchka, *Pyat' mesyatsev Sotsialisticheskoi Sovetskoi Latvii* (Moscow 1919), p. 68, pp. 81-82.
2. Stuchka, *Pyat'*, p. 160.
3. Swain, 'Disillusioning', pp. 670-671.
4. This summary of Bolshevik policy is mainly taken from Adams, *Ukraine*, chapter 4; see also Michael Malet, *Nestor Makhno in the Russian Civil War* (Macmillan Basingstoke 1982), p. 134 and P. Arshinov, *History of the Makhnovist Movement, 1918-20* (Freedom Press London 1987), p. 80.
5. Adams, *Ukraine*, pp. 228-234, p. 266; Lenin's response is in *Collected Works*, Vol. 44, p. 213.
6. Lenin, *Collected Works*, Vol. 29, p. 159.
7. Lenin, *Collected Works*, Vol. 29, p. 214, p. 217.
8. For a full account of the Don Rebellion, see Brian Murphy, 'The Don Rebellion, March-June 1919' in *Revolutionary Russia*, Vol. 6, No. 2, 1993, pp. 315-350.
9. V. Danilov et al. (eds), *Filip Mironov: Tikhii Don v 1917-1921 gg.* (Mezhdunarodnyi fond 'Demokratiya', Moscow 1997), pp. 5-12; for Stalin and Mironov, see p. 77.
10. Murphy, *Don*, pp. 322-327.
11. Danilov, *Mironov*, p. 160, p. 177.
12. Danilov, *Mironov*, p. 162-163, p. 187, p. 317; for the mutilated bodies, see Butt, *Documents*, p. 52.

13. Danilov, *Mironov*, p. 155.
14. Danilov, *Mironov*, p. 169, p. 172
15. For the start of the rebellion, see Murphy, *Don*, p. 326; for the rebels' demands, see Danilov, *Mironov*, p. 159.
16. Murphy, *Don*, p. 346.
17. Danilov, *Mironov*, p. 177.
18. Muphy, *Don*, pp. 333-337.
19. Adams, *Ukraine*, p. 304.
20. Adams, *Ukraine*, p. 313, p. 335.
21. Butt, *Documents*, p. 84.
22. Adams, *Ukraine*, p. 327, p. 336, p. 338.
23. Arshinov, *History*, p. 53, pp. 80-89.
24. Arshinov, *History*, pp. 95-98.
25. For Antonov Ovseenko and the Kharkov *Izvestiya*, see Malet, *Makhno*, p. 33; for his report to the Ukrainian government, see Butt, *Documents*, p. 87.
26. Arshinov, *History*, pp. 105-114.
27. Arshinov, *History*, p. 127; for Makhno's retreat and the pharse 'anarchist kulak debauchery', see Malet, *Makhno*, p. 36, p. 38.
28. Arshinov, *History*, pp. 133-136, p. 141.
29. Lenin, *Collected Works*, Vol. 44, p. 215.
30. Mawdsley, *Civil War*, pp. 171-174; Lincoln, *Red*, pp. 214-217.
31. Butt, *Documents*, p. 81.
32. Robert McNeal, *Stalin: Man and Ruler*, (Macmillan Basingstoke 1988), p. 59.
33. Gordon Brook-Shepherd, *Iron Maze*, (Macmillan Basingstoke 1998). The work of Dukes is described in chapter eight. The Bolshevik angle is given in N. E Kakurin, *Kak srazhalas' revolyutsiya* (Moscow 1990), Vol. 2, p. 195.
34. F. Benvenuti, *The Bolsheviks and the Red Army, 1918-22* (Cambridge University Press 1988), p. 132.
35. Butt, *Documents*, p. 103.
36. Benvenuti, *Red Army*, p. 135.
37. This complex affair is described in Benvenuti, *Red Army*, pp. 133-135, and Kakurin, *Kak srazhalas'*, Vol. 2, pp. 216-250.
38. Kakurin, *Kak*, Vol. 2, p. 228 et seq.; Lincoln, *Red*, p. 222; Benvenuti, *The Red Army*, p. 134 et seq.
39. For Selivachev's arrest, see Butt, *Documents*, p. 105; otherwise Mawdsley, *Civil War*, pp. 175-177.
40. M. Aten, *Last Train Over Rostov Bridge* (Cassel, London 1962), pp. 69-77.
41. Danilov, *Mironov*, p. 220, p. 243.
42. Danilov, *Mironov*, p. 270, p. 293, p. 380.
43. Danilov, *Mironov*, pp. 314-316, p. 334.
44. See the official report into the rebellion, reproduced in Danilov, *Mironov*, pp. 353-370.
45. Danilov, *Mironov*, pp. 374-376; p. 387, p. 403

46. For the Mamontov raid and Trotsky's response, see Mawdsley, *Civil War*, p. 220 and Lincoln, *Red*, pp. 224-226; for the report, see Butt, *Documents*, p. 63.

47. This summary is taken from Peter Kenez, *The Civil War in South Russia, 1919-20: the Defeat of the Whites* (University of California Press 1977) chapter 3.

48. Kenez, *South Russia*, pp. 86-92.

49. The antisemitism of Denikin's forces is dicussed in detail in Kenez, *South Russia*, pp. 166-177; the quoted passage is p. 172.

50. The Kiev labour union is covered in Kenez, *South Russia*, p. 108 et seq.; for labour policy in general see pp. 103-107.

51. H. Kuromiya, *Freedom and Terror in the Donbas* (Cambridge University Press, 1998), pp. 104-105.

52. Kenez, *South Russia*, pp. 157-158.

4 White Defeat; Green/Red Stalemate

1. Brovkin, *Behind*, p. 175; K.V. Gusev, *Partiya Eserov: ot melko-burzhuaznogo revolyutsirizma k kontrrevolyutsii* (Moscow 1975), p. 300; K.V. Gusev & Kh.A. Yeritsyan, *Ot soglashatel'stva k kontrrevolyutsii* (Moscow 1968), p. 355.

2. Gusev, *Ot soglashatel'stva*, pp. 355-360.

3. K. Burevoi, *Kolchakovshchina* (Moscow 1919), pp. 36-40.

4. Danilov, *Mironov*, p. 416, p. 430, p. 433, p. 436, p. 457, p. 459.

5. Arshinov, *History*, pp. 141-147.

6. A.D. Rumyantsev, 'Moi boevye druzya latyshi' in *Latyshskiye strelki v bor'be za sovetskuyu vlast' v 1917-20 gg.: vospominaniya i dokumenty* (Riga 1962), p. 387; Mawdsley, *Civil War*, p. 200.

7. Mawdsley, *Civil War*, p. 202.

8. For the anarchist view, see Arshinov, *History*, p. 113; for Makhno in Moscow, see N. Makhno, *Vospominaniya* (Mosow, Respublika, 1992), p. 155; otherwise Malet, *Makhno*, p. 121, p. 166. Note however that Antonov-Ovseekno's report of May 1919 noted 'that they do not care for the Left SRs', Butt, *Documents*, p. 87.

9. Arshinov, *History*, p. 154, pp. 161-162; Malet, *Makhno*, p. 149.

10. A.B. Murphy, *The Russian Civil War: Primary Sources* (Macmillan, Basingstoke, 2000), pp. 190-191.

11. Arshinov, *History*, p. 163-164, p. 265.

12. This summary is taken from N. Voronovich, 'Mezh dvukh ognei (zapiski zelenogo)' *Arkhiv Russkoi Revolyutsii*, No. 7, 1922.

13. Voronovich, 'Zapiski zelenogo', p. 111, p. 123.

14. V. Favitskii, 'Zelenaya armiya v Chernomor'ye', *Proletarskaya Revolyutsiya*, No. 8, 1924, p. 48.

15. Voronovich, 'Zapiski zelenogo', pp. 118-126; M. Dobranistskii, 'Zelenye partizany', *Proletarskaya Revolyutsiya*, No. 8, 1924, p. 75.

16. Voronovich, 'Zapiski zelenogo', pp. 127-131.

17. Voronovich, 'Zapiski zelenogo', pp. 138-143.
18. Voronovich, 'Zapiski zelenogo' pp. 146-148; Favistskii, 'Zelenaya armiya', pp. 64-65.
19. Voronovich, 'Zapiski zelenogo', pp. 153-163, p. 171-174.
20. Smele, *Siberia*, pp. 552-553.
21. Smele, *Siberia*, pp. 555-556.
22. For the Autonomous Group of Siberian SRs, see Smele, *Siberia*, n. 14, p. 556; Gajda's revolt is summarised on pp. 564-570.
23. Smele, *Siberia*, pp. 573-580, p. 612.
24. *The Manchester Guardian*, 20 July 1920; the paper's special correspondent was the British liaison officer Leo Steveni.
25. For the Irkutsk insurrection, see Smele, *Siberia*, pp.608-626.
26. *The Manchester Guardian*, 7 July 1920.
27. Pereira, *White Siberia*, p. 144, pp. 157-159.
28. J.M. Meijer, *The Trotsky Papers*, (Mouton & Co, The Hague, 1964), Vol. 2, p. 47.
29. Novomeysky, *Siberian Life*, p. 309.
30. K.V. Gusev, *Partiya Eserov*, pp. 313-315; Meijer, *The Trotsky Papers*, Vol. 2, pp. 115-117.
31. The Labour Armies are discussed in more detail in Butt, *Documents*, chapter 4.
32. Robert Service, *Lenin: A Political Life* (Macmillan, Basingstoke 1995), Vol. 3, pp. 117-122.
33. Mawdsley, *Civil War*, pp. 268-271; Lincoln, *Red Victory*, pp. 434-448.
34. Lincoln, *Red Victory*, p. 438; Voronovich, 'Zapsiki zelenogo', p. 182.
35. Arshinov, *History*, pp. 176-191.
36. T. Osipova, 'Peasant Rebellions: Origin, Scope, Dynamics and Consequences' in Brovkin, *The Bolsheviks*, p. 172.
37. Arshinov, *History*, pp. 196-206; for the 'free soviets' broadcast, see Jonathan Aves, *Workers against Lenin: Labour Protest and the Bolshevik Dictatorship* (London, I.B. Tauris 1996) p. 172.
38. Murphy, *Primary Sources*, p. 220, p. 224, p. 226.
39. Murphy, *Primary Sources*, p. 237; Arshinov, *History*, p. 204.
40. For Mironov's attitude to Makhno, see Danilov, *Mironov*, p. 517; for his dismissal, arrest and execution, see p. 588 et seq.
41. Danilov, *Mironov*, p. 642.
42. Arshinov, *History*, pp. 201-206.
43. This summary of the Antonov rebellion is taken from the classic account O.H. Radkey, *The Unknown Civil War in Soviet Russia* (Hoover Institution, Stanford, 1976).
44. Radkey, *Unknown*, p. 143.
45. D. Dugarm, 'Peasant Wars in Tambov Province' in V.N. Brovkin, *The Bolsheviks in Russian Society* (Yale University Press 1997), p. 185.
46. S.A Yesikov & V.V. Kanishchev, '"Antonovskii NEP": organizatsiya i deyatel'nost' Soyuza Trudovogo Krestyanstva Tambovskoi gubernii 1920-21' in *Otechestvennaya Istoriya*, No. 4 ,1993, pp. 62-71.

47. Dugarm, 'Peasant Wars', p. 189 et seq.; Radkey, *Unknown*, p. 347.

48. N.G.O Pereira, 'The Partisan Movement in Western Siberia' in *Jahrbuecher fuer Geschichte Ost-Europas*, No. 1, 1990, p. 96; Osipova, 'Peasant Rebellions', pp. 169-170.

49. For the peasant revolt of Western Siberia, see V.V. Moskovskii, 'Vosstanie krest'yan v Zapadnoi Sibiri v 1921 godu' *Voprosy istorii,* No. 6, 1998, pp. 46-63.

50. Service, *Lenin*, Vol, 3, pp. 168-171.

51. Aves, *Workers*, p. 140 et seq.

5 Red Victory: Causes and Consequences

1. Mawdsley, *Civil War*, p. 181.

2. Kakurin, *Kak*, Vol. 2, p. 26.

3. Lincoln, *Red Victory*, p. 224, p. 442.

4. Voronovich, 'Zapiski zelenogo', pp. 172-174.

5. Kakurin, *Kak*, Vol. 2, p. 27.

6. Benvenuti, *The Red Army*, p. 214.

7. Benvenuti, *The Red Army*, pp. 25-26, p. 53 et seq.

8. Benvenuti, *The Red Army*, p. 79.

9. Benvenuti, *The Bolsheviks*, pp. 112-117.

10. Butt, *Documents*, p.64, p. 73.

11. Butt, *Documents*, p. 61.

12. Butt, *Documents*, p. 73, p. 75, p. 96, p. 101.

13. Butt, *Documents*, p. 97, p. 111.

14. Graziosi, *Soviet Peasant War*, p. 22.

15. Butt, *Documents*, p. 89.

16. Lenin, *Collected Works*, Vol. 28, p. 209.

17. M. Jansen, *A Show Trial Under Lenin* (Martinus Nijhoff, the Hague, 1982), pp. 11-12.

18. Jansen, *Show Trial*, pp. 14-16.

19. Jansen, *Show Trial*, p. 51, p. 58, pp. 76-78.

20. This short summary is distilled from Jansen's detailed account, which begins on p. 61

21. Jansen, *Show Trial*, p. 176.

22. For the Assembly of Factory Delegates, see Brovkin, *The Mensheviks*, p. 162 *et seq*.

23. Stalin's time in Tsaritsyn is described in R. Argenbright, 'Red Tsaritsyn: Precursor of Stalinist Terror' *Revolutionary Russia*, No. 2, 1991.

24. Kaganovich's time in Nizhny Novgorod is described by E.A. Rees in an unpublished paper 'Red Terror and Party Rule in Nizhny Novgorod: Lazar Kaganovich's Big Secret' given at the Centre for Russian and East European Studies, University of Birmingham, December 1997.

25. Kirov's time in Astrakhan is described in J. Biggart, 'The Astrakhan Rebellion: An Episode in the Career of S.M. Kirov', *Slavonic and East European Review* Vol. 54, No. 2, 1976.
26. Butt, *Documents*, p. 107.
27. J. Hasek, *The Red Commissar* (Abacus-Sphere, 1983), p. 36.

Index

References in bold denote an illustration